BLOCKCHAIN
GOVERNANCE

The MIT Press Essential Knowledge Series

A complete list of books in this series can be found online at
https://mitpress.mit.edu/books/series/mit-press-essential-knowledge-series.

BLOCKCHAIN GOVERNANCE

PRIMAVERA DE FILIPPI,
WESSEL REIJERS, AND
MORSHED MANNAN

The MIT Press | Cambridge, Massachusetts | London, England

The MIT Press would like to thank the anonymous peer reviewers who provided comments on drafts of this book. The generous work of academic experts is essential for establishing the authority and quality of our publications. We acknowledge with gratitude the contributions of these otherwise uncredited readers.

This book was set in Chaparral Pro by New Best-set Typesetters Ltd. Printed and bound in the United States of America.

Library of Congress Cataloging-in-Publication Data

Names: De Filippi, Primavera, author. | Reijers, Wessel, 1989- author. | Mannan, Morshed, 1990- author.
Title: Blockchain governance / Primavera De Filippi, Wessel Reijers, and Morshed Mannan.
Description: Cambridge, Massachusetts : The MIT Press, [2024] | Series: The MIT Press essential knowledge series | Includes bibliographical references and index.
Identifiers: LCCN 2023053314 (print) | LCCN 2023053315 (ebook) | ISBN 9780262549059 (paperback) | ISBN 9780262379861 (epub) | ISBN 9780262379878 (pdf)
Subjects: LCSH: Blockchains (Databases)—Government policy. | Internet governance. | Technology and law.
Classification: LCC QA76.9.B56 D455 2024 (print) | LCC QA76.9.B56 (ebook) | DDC 005.75/88—dc23/eng/20240215
LC record available at https://lccn.loc.gov/2023053314
LC ebook record available at https://lccn.loc.gov/2023053315

10 9 8 7 6 5 4 3 2 1

CONTENTS

SERIES FOREWORD

The MIT Press Essential Knowledge series offers accessible, concise, beautifully produced pocket-size books on topics of current interest. Written by leading thinkers, the books in this series deliver expert overviews of subjects that range from the cultural and the historical to the scientific and the technical.

In today's era of instant information gratification, we have ready access to opinions, rationalizations, and superficial descriptions. Much harder to come by is the foundational knowledge that informs a principled understanding of the world. Essential Knowledge books fill that need. Synthesizing specialized subject matter for nonspecialists and engaging critical topics through fundamentals, each of these compact volumes offers readers a point of access to complex ideas.

In the spring of 2023, when we were wrapping up the book that you are now reading, a remarkable gathering happened on the coast of the Adriatic, in a resort near Tivat in Montenegro. A few hundred people, including two of us, assembled in Zuzalu, a pop-up city initiated by (among others) the visionary founder of the Ethereum blockchain, Vitalik Buterin. People from all kinds of backgrounds—blockchain engineers and computer scientists, artists and philosophers, entrepreneurs and lawyers, and so forth—came together to discuss a variety of topics, from artificial intelligence to human longevity and the future of the nation-state.

Zuzalu was home to a variety of ideologies and interests. Some residents were involved in establishing zones that were beyond the jurisdiction of any state's legal system so that they could test life extension treatments. For them, Zuzalu was a tentative manifestation of the "network state," a concept introduced by Silicon Valley tech entrepreneur Balaji Srinivasan, which envisions dispersed networks of people and capital ultimately gaining recognition as sovereign entities. The idea of the network state builds on libertarian visions that have a long history. This ranges from the secretive Galt's Gulch, an enclave in Ayn Rand's *Atlas Shrugged* that survives the collapse of ineffective government, to seaborne platforms in the high seas that, according to Peter Thiel, would allow humankind to escape politics and secure spaces safe for capitalism and freedom. Yet, for many other residents, the appeal of Zuzalu was the opportunity it provided for imagining postcapitalist futures within existing nation-states and developing new tools and practices for societal transformation. In this sense, its ethos was more like Calafou, a self-managed eco-industrial colony in Catalonia where Buterin spent time in the months leading to the drafting of the Ethereum white paper.

A shared interest of Zuzalu residents was that the world's established institutions, and governance as we now know it, are not the only tools we have to govern society. We don't need to be citizens of nation-states with defined territories and the rights and duties that traditional citizenship entails. Instead, we can move between "digital tribes" and "network archipelagos," which may exist anywhere, at any time. We would have multiple citizenships and belong to multiple networks, all based on our personal interests that would sometimes converge and sometimes diverge. For some, the network state promises a do-over, an opportunity to dismantle the regulations, red tape, and bureaucracy that characterize modern states and to rebuild societies as bastions of human autonomy, political liberty, and economic freedom. For others, the network state is a buzzword that is being used to market wild colonial enterprises, from Central America to the South Pacific, that operate without democratic oversight, threaten hard-won statutory protections, and place local communities and institutions at risk. In this way, some have tried to turn Puerto Rico into a crypto tax haven and test bed for experimenting with new technologies, while leeching on to the local population.

In contrast, other visions do not see *exit* as the central organizing principle of global governance but rather *interdependence*. In the sessions two of us convened at Zuzalu, we discussed the ideas of "coordi-nations" and "new network sovereignties," which can leverage blockchains and other technologies (e.g., for identity management) but are primarily intended to foster human cooperation at local and global levels through the cultivation of shared values, participatory governance, and the mutualization of resources. Instead of privatizing public goods or gnawing away at the sovereignty of the state, coordi-nations would coexist with the state and meet needs that states do not. Whatever your views on this subject may be, for us Zuzalu was akin to an ancient Greek agora, a place where people could freely exchange utopian ideas through agreement and contestation.

In short, the future of governance was a core theme of the discussions that took place in the assemblies and salons at Zuzalu. It is also a subject that we collectively, and individually, have been researching for several years within various contexts. While blockchain communities love to experiment and speculate about the modes of governance of the future—invariably powered by blockchain—we wanted to put ourselves at the intersection of theory and practice. On the one hand, researching blockchain inevitably means getting one's hands dirty and engaging with the world of practice—for instance, by applying ethnographic methods and actively engaging with blockchain communities. While we do not have a significant stake in any of the blockchain projects that feature in this book, we have embedded ourselves in blockchain communities as a way of conducting research, to understand this world and its working from the inside out. On the other hand, writing this book required us to maintain a critical distance. Delving into political and legal theory, we engaged with old and contemporary ideas derived from the literature to critically assess the claims of blockchain proponents concerning the revolutionary new forms of governance this technology offers and the sweeping implications it may have. What does it mean, we ask, for blockchain technology to be "trustless" and "alegal"? Are these technical systems immune to political challenges like states of emergency, and can the governance of these systems ever be made legitimate?

At the time of writing this preface, in March 2024, the ecosystem of blockchain technology seems to have moved to a new stage. In the wake of the scandals surrounding some of the major exchanges, FTX and Binance, and the spectacular fall of industry-leading figures like Sam Bankman-Fried, a crypto winter set in. After years of attention and hype, blockchain technology is somewhat out of the limelight, with the big boom in artificial intelligence applications dominating global attention. This, however, has also opened up two new pathways for the maturity of blockchain technology and blockchain governance. First, as Buterin stressed on multiple occasions, without the burden of the speculative bubble, blockchain projects may finally return (or perhaps, progress) to their roots in cypherpunk ideology. Perhaps more generally, without having to commit to a particular ideology, blockchain communities and policymakers may find the space and time to reflect on the deeper political and legal issues faced by blockchain ecosystems. We hope that this book will provide a starting point for these reflections. Second, and relatedly, ongoing legislative and regulatory activity has provided greater clarity about the rules applicable to this technology and the crypto-industry and has provided insight into the attitudes of policymakers toward both. On the one hand, through legislation such as the EU's recent Markets in Crypto-Assets regulation, we have greater certainty about the terms under which certain crypto asset services can be provided. On the other hand, new regulations or the application of existing laws may be poorly suited for the development of this technological innovation or even ineffective in achieving their intended purposes. Cases concerning economic sanctions on blockchain-based software systems and the liability of members of decentralized autonomous organizations (DAOs) that are discussed in this book reveal some of the shortcomings of the prevailing "regulation by enforcement" approach. Instead, we elaborate on a "regulation by governance" approach that seeks to meet important public policy objectives through technical (e.g., new governance technologies) and social means (e.g., social norms cultivation) that are compatible with the particular features of blockchain technology and the industry as a whole. As regulatory activity continues to grow apace, we hope that the concerns and recommendations we mention also receive consideration.

This book results from years of close collaboration, and we, the authors, have equally contributed to the research and writing of this manuscript. We would like to take this opportunity to thank the many people without whom this book would not have been possible. First, these include members of the ERC project BlockchainGov, especially Kelsie Nabben, Sofia Cossar, Silke Noa, and Tara Merk. Second, we have gained valuable input from colleagues, most notably Nathan Schneider, Eric Alston, Liav Orgad, Ellie Rennie, and Jason Potts. We would not have had the time and resources to finish the book without the generous support of the European Research Council (grant number 865856 under the European Union's Horizon

2020 Research and Innovation Programme) and the supportive environments of CERSA, the Berkman Klein Center for Internet & Society at Harvard University, the European University Institute, and the University of Vienna. Finally, we would like to thank our families and friends for their patience and support while we worked on this manuscript.

NEW CAMBRIAN EXPLOSION

We have sealed ourselves away behind our money,
growing inward, generating a seamless universe of self.
—William Gibson, *Neuromancer*[1]

Cambrian Explosion

In 1992, Francis Fukuyama announced the "end of history," signaling the end of an evolutionary process in terms of governance structures.[2] The world had found a lasting collection of stable forms of governance: representative democracies, capitalist firms, and civil society organizations, such as nonprofit associations and foundations. In a Hegelian vein, Fukuyama believed that liberal democracy was the endpoint of a long historical progress, the arrival of the Absolute Spirit. His message was symptomatic of the optimistic spirit of his time. Just three years before, the Iron Curtain had fallen and America had emerged as the global hegemon, condemning the Soviet experiment to the dustbin of history. An increasing number of countries adopted liberal-democratic means of government and embraced capitalism, and authoritarianism was in apparent decline.

Two thousand years earlier, the philosopher Aristotle painted a very different picture about the possibility of realizing an ideal system of governance. Criticizing his mentor Plato, he lamented the preoccupation of philosophers with the "ideal state" such as Plato's utopian vision of a republic governed by philosopher-citizens. Instead, he believed, one should start inquiring into politics empirically, by simply looking around. Ancient Greece had witnessed a unique historical moment with the emergence of the polis, the city state. Rather than being characterized by uniformity, city states were extremely diverse.

In *The Politics*, Aristotle surveyed the actual constitutions of the city states and the hugely diverse ways in which they organize property rights, establish citizenship rights, and make decisions. Phaleas of Chalcedon, for instance, proposed an extremely egalitarian property regime, where the rich would donate their inheritance to the poor.[3] Hippodamus of Miletus tried to implement a class-based system, where the population was divided into three groups: craftsmen, farmers, and soldiers.[4] Sparta added an interesting gender dimension to the governance of its city state: while men went off to war, women were often in charge of ruling the city, much to Aristotle's dismay.[5] Carthage had a system in which the kings were not destined to rule by birthright but were elected based on their merit and wealth.[6] Aristotle also recounted the great innovations brought about by Solon, who abolished the oligarchy, put an end to some forms of slavery, and established "ancestral democracy." Law courts in Athens were elected by lottery rather than appointed on aristocratic grounds.[7]

At that time, ancient Greece experienced a "Cambrian explosion" of forms of governance. This is a metaphorical reference to an interval of a few million years about 500 million years ago in which the geological records show an extremely quick and prolific diversification of organic life. Biological evolution, it appears, is not linear; it moves dynamically between greater diversification and greater homogenization. The same, at times, applies to the ways humans govern their societies. As Graeber and Wengrow recently argued, our modern understanding of how governance evolved is still very much in line with Fukuyama's thesis.[8] Coming from the likes of Hobbes and Rousseau, we often believe in a linear progression of political evolution, from a (peaceful or brutish) state of nature to the sovereign nation state. Yet, historical records often disagree. Prehistory was teeming with "social experiments . . .

resembling a carnival parade of political forms."[9] Examples include popular assemblies in ancient Mesopotamia and urban democracies in ancient cities in Middle America. And such diversity recurs in the historical records. The Italian city states, like Siena and Bologna, saw the emergence of communes with citizen assemblies and great variety in their constitutions.[10] Similarly, the wild growth of utopian communities in the United States in the nineteenth century was highly diversified: some of them were deeply conservative and authoritarian, while others established surprisingly progressive governance principles, like sexual freedom and gender equality.[11]

Certainly, many factors play a role in Cambrian explosions of human governance, and one of these is undeniably technology. Ancient Greece and its many colonies would not have been imaginable without agricultural innovations and revolutionary ways of ship building, which produced ships like the trireme. The Italian city states thrived because of the increase in trade, the result of naval innovations, the building of infrastructure, and new financial tools such as double-entry bookkeeping. And nineteenth-century utopian experiments, like Robert Owen's New Harmony, would not have been conceivable without the industrial technology that enabled transatlantic long-distance travel and communication. Technology has also played an important role in establishing new, often utopian, political visions that would inform the shaping of actual constitutions. As Lewis Mumford argued, visions of a "collective human machine" were considered political blueprints for how to govern society[12]—be they the slave-machine that built the pyramids in Egypt, offering a blueprint for absolute kingly rule, or the sailor-machine that navigated the trireme across the Aegean Sea, whose steersman or *kybernetes* provided the blueprint for the guardian class of philosopher-citizens. In a similar vein, the role of mechanical technologies like the astronomical clock contributed to shaping Hobbes's idea of the sovereign as a spirit-machine, while the steam engine participated in the shaping of utopian dreamscapes like the ones established by Saint-Simon.

This new role of technology is becoming increasingly explicit in the twenty-first century. Rather than being an enabling factor, or an inspiration for utopian ideas of governance, technology is gaining political force and is becoming a form of governance in and of itself. This was not yet the case in the mechanical age, for—as Newton believed—even the perfect clockwork that was the universe needed a prime mover other than itself: the watchmaker (i.e., God). Since the invention of the Turing machine, however, symbolic machines now share a faculty that was deemed exclusively human, namely the ability to make decisions. Today, machine-made decisions are all around us, nudging us, guiding us, and sometimes even coercing us. Recommendation algorithms decide what content or ads we get to see online, while content moderation systems decide what will be hidden from view.

Yet, as with Newton's clockwork universe, behind these machine-powered decision-making systems sit a group of "prime movers" who do not qualify as gods but as humans made of flesh and blood, be they Mark Zuckerberg or Xi Jinping. This book is about a new cybernetic watch that purports to push aside its watchmaker(s) and whose first instantiation was the cryptocurrency, Bitcoin. Three decades after Fukuyama's thesis, blockchain technologies are propelling a Cambrian explosion of new governance systems. Radically new governance concepts are being brought to the forefront: from distributed consensus to decentralized autonomous organizations (DAOs), with many others on the horizon.

These radical new forms of governance do not emerge out of a vacuum but instead ride on a wave of sociotechnical imaginaries that interpret technological advancements in light of speculative science fiction and political visions. The idea of cyberspace—a virtual, open-ended matrix having its roots in arcade games—itself emerged in science fiction, famously being coined in William Gibson's *Neuromancer*.[13] In a similar vein, Neal Stephenson, in *The Diamond Age*, imagined that the information age would bring a kind of distributed republic or tribe, called a "phyle."[14] Technology is abundant in this world, but the protocol produces artificial scarcity. People can opt in to phyles, which are run as peer-to-peer networks, depending on their affinity, such as religion or ideology. More recently, in *Too Like the Lightning*, the first book in the Terra Ignota series, Ada Palmer imagined the ruling powers of the future as "Hives."[15] In the series, these Hives enable voluntary citizenships, incorporating different languages, customs, and governance regimes, with new technologies fueling prosperity for some and surveillance and censorship for many others. These networked, distributed political communities are the early visions of "cloud communities,"[16] an idea that is now fueling serious discussions about the future of global citizenship.

Such visions, emerging from science fiction, suggest that a different world, with a different philosophy and a different politics, is possible. Whether this world is benign or evil remains an open question. Yet, there seems to be a movement visible in these sociotechnical imaginaries, one that resonates with the world we actually live in. First, there is the growing importance of technology. In the 1950s, people still imagined planetary civilization to be run quite similarly to their own places and times; we have moved to imaginaries of brain-chip-empowered hive-minds that coordinate economic activities through voluntary peer-to-peer networks. Second, there is a move away from what Palmer described as the "old spider," the nation state. Our political existence, we imagine, is deterritorializing, dematerializing, and moving into the boundless expanse of cyberspace. We are both everywhere and nowhere, but political power and physical bodies still persist, generating divisions between the haves and the have nots and reminding us of the temporality of our own existence. Third, as anticipated by Marshall McLuhan, we reach back into the distant past to understand our present and envision our possibilities for the future.[17] Stephenson's phyle was derived from the idea of a tribe in ancient Greece. To put it in the words of Palmer's protagonist, "whether you are my contemporary still awed by the new order, or an historian gazing back at my Twenty-Fifth Century as remotely as I gaze back on the Eighteenth, you will find yourself more fluent in the language of the past than you imagined; we all are."[18] We need, as Carugati and Schneider put it, a new practice of "governance archeology."[19]

These three developments—the revolutionary role of technology, moving away from the nation state, and a revival of political ideas from the past—have fueled not only science fiction but also concrete developments in technology. Already in the 1970s, influential figures like Steward Brand used their imaginations to fuse drugs, advanced electronic networks, and ideals of living in primitive communities to fuel the vision that powered Silicon Valley and its Californian Ideology.[20] Later, John Perry Barlow extended this vision to the digital world, when he imagined cyberspace (a term borrowed from science fiction) as a frictionless new world that would bring equality and abundance in the digital realm. For all the prowess of their speculations, old-fashioned human organizations still sat firmly behind the wheel of Brand's and Barlow's technological utopias until October 31, 2008.

On that day, the publication of the Bitcoin white paper established a new technological infrastructure—blockchain technology—through which people can interact and transact in a peer-to-peer manner. Blockchain technology is a new type of economic and political institution that works outside of the existing political fabric made up of trusted intermediaries,[21] be they either state agencies, corporations, or civil society organizations. It operates as a distributed processing network (or "world computer") that is not owned or controlled by anyone and whose records are immutable. Initially created to realize the political vision of a small group of visionaries, known as the "cypherpunks," blockchain technology has, since its inception, moved in many new directions and today constitutes a new basis for transactions, rulemaking, and decision-making.

Why Blockchain Governance?

This book is about blockchain governance, which covers the regulation and governance *of* and *by* blockchain technology. It is concerned with a wide range of issues, from how policymakers may respond to challenges raised by blockchain, via how blockchain developers can grapple with tensions in protocol design, to how fundamental principles like immutability both enable and hinder governance alternatives. Blockchain governance captures the dual aspects of governance *by* the technology (*on-chain* governance) and governance *of* the technology (*off-chain* governance). The dynamic between these two aspects of blockchain governance is a major theme of this book and will reappear throughout the chapters—for instance, in exploring the tension between the concepts of trust and confidence in an ostensibly "trustless" network and in assessing the impact of exogenous and endogenous pressures in shaping perceptions about the legitimacy of blockchain governance.

In the following chapters, we find ourselves in the footsteps of Aristotle, who in his time witnessed a proliferation of new forms of governance in the Greek city states: from tyrannies to aristocracies, oligarchies, and democracies. It is in this context that the disciplines of law and political science first emerged to reflect on the questions of governance: What should a government look like? What is the role of a citizen and of the state? How does political change occur? How can political communities improve a citizen's happiness and well-being? How should citizens be encouraged to be just and virtuous? Now, blockchain communities around the world are experimenting with different

Blockchain governance captures the dual aspects of governance *by* the technology (*on-chain* governance) and governance *of* the technology (*off-chain* governance).

consensus algorithms, innovative voting systems, dispute resolution systems, and community covenants that are meant to act like written constitutions. And similar questions of governance arise: Should blockchain communities adhere to the "rule of code" or allow human interference in the administration of the protocol? Should a blockchain governance system adhere to democratic principles, or could it adopt a plutocratic form of governance? How should blockchain communities preserve the polycentric nature of public permissionless blockchain networks?

Answering these questions is not straightforward. As Vili Lehdonvirta argued in 2016, blockchain governance is inherently a "paradox." He asked, Isn't it the point of blockchain technologies to obviate the need for (human) governance? And if it is not, and (human) governance is needed, why is a blockchain required at all, if people are going to ultimately trust a third party?[22] The experience of the subsequent years has revealed that as the crypto economy has gone through boom and bust cycles, the importance of governance in particular has only grown. Indeed, good and effective governance has been predicted to be an important competitive feature of blockchain systems.[23]

Why is it important to investigate blockchain governance? First, blockchain technology has become a consequential force in the world. Back in 2010, Bitcoin was still unknown to most people, its nascent community celebrated when someone used the cryptocurrency to buy a pizza. Only one decade later, blockchain technology has disrupted virtually every sector. It has become a trillion-dollar industry, with millions of people around the world developing Web3 applications, investing in new crypto projects, or chatting about the latest crypto crisis with colleagues over coffee. Blockchain has become a topic discussed by heads of state, central bankers, and the CEOs of the world's largest companies. This growing relevance of blockchain technology automatically raises concerns of governance. Blockchain developers have started asking questions about their relationship with regulators, while policymakers have started to explore new pathways to formulating effective regulations. To do this wisely, an understanding of blockchain governance, in terms of its promises and challenges, is indispensable.

Second, blockchain is surrounded by significant legal and regulatory uncertainty. Even though states have started formulating policies and regulations for blockchain technologies, several of these efforts are often plagued by both a lack of expertise and a lack of foresight. Blockchain technology confronts us with the Collingridge dilemma. On the one hand, as long as the technology is still emerging, its consequences will be uncertain and therefore difficult to control. For instance, The DAO attack in 2016 (discussed in chapter 5) had significant impact but was unforeseen—and even unintelligible—for most policymakers. On the other hand, as soon as blockchain technology gets entrenched in established institutions or ways of life, its consequences might be predictable, but the technology will be hard to control or steer. Projects are currently underway that aim to make blockchain the underlying technology for the governance of social media, global supply chain management, and global identity registries. Whether these projects succeed remains to be seen, but if they do, their consequences will be widespread, and it will become increasingly difficult to address or revert them. An important way to deal with this legal uncertainty is to analyze the potential regulation and governance challenges through the lens of legal and political theory, which is what this book intends to do.

Third, blockchain is increasingly challenging our conceptual understanding of law and regulation. It does so in different ways. To start, it challenges and extends the concerns raised by scholars of Internet governance, related to the adage that "code is law." While most people and organizations operating on the Internet continue to be subject to state laws, blockchain adds a new dynamic by promoting the autonomy of code. Blockchain systems purport to generate their own legal reality that is independent of the will of human participants interacting through them—and can therefore not be instrumentalized by centralized authorities—which in this book is captured as the rule of code, by way of analogy to the "rule of law." The rules enshrined in blockchain-based systems are such that they share certain features with state and nonstate constitutional law systems. Moreover, by operating transnationally, blockchain systems are, to some extent, detached from the sovereignty of particular nation-states. They thus bring to the forefront a challenge earlier identified by scholars in the fields of societal, global, and digital constitutionalism, namely that constitutional orders are not limited to the sovereignty of nation-states. Instead, transnational organizations, large platforms, and now also quasi-autonomous blockchain systems generate constitutional orders that are simultaneously compatible and in tension with established laws and regulations (discussed in chapter 7).

Fourth, because of their inherent characteristics, blockchain systems introduce new modes of governance that urge us to rethink established political concepts. Political philosophy has revolved around certain key questions concerning political authority and sovereignty (e.g., what is the basis of sovereign power?), legitimacy (e.g., why do citizens accept and obey a system of governance?), and democracy (e.g., what are good procedures for democratic decision-making, how are citizens represented by political bodies?). Blockchain governance adds new dynamics to each of these questions, thereby also challenging established political concepts.

For instance, while in traditional organizations authority is ultimately vested in human decision makers, the authority of blockchain-based systems is vested in a (purportedly) immutable code-based protocol, which will execute as planned regardless of the intent of the parties involved. Besides, even where human governance is involved, the pseudonymity inherent in most blockchain networks precludes an important set of governance dynamics (including the "one person, one vote" principle in traditional democracies), ultimately favoring more plutocratic or meritocratic modes of governance. Legitimacy also increasingly acquires a crucial role in blockchain systems, not as a means to justify the coercive actions of a sovereign—as in more traditional centralized governance structures—but as a mechanism to ensure loyalty to a system that is ultimately driven by voluntary participation. Finally, to the extent that blockchain systems can be regarded as "polycentric" governance systems (i.e., systems characterized by multiple overlapping centers of decision-making under an overarching shared set of rules), new questions emerge concerning the appropriate scale(s) at which these networks should (or can) be governed—from the individual core developer, via the multinational cryptocurrency exchange, to the globe-spanning technical infrastructure of the network itself.

For some scholars, corporate governance offers a more appropriate theoretical lenses with which to analyze blockchain systems than political governance, as these systems rely on "voluntary cooperation" (like corporations) and act "more like markets than hierarchies."[24] This is in contrast to the involuntary cooperation inherent in states, where the state's capacity to coerce makes political concepts of legitimacy and deliberation more important. From a corporate governance perspective, the potential failure of a contract or problem of trust between network participants (e.g., from users to core developers) can be viewed as issues of bounded rationality, opportunism, or maladaptation (e.g., contractual arrangements no longer effective after real-world changes). Consequently, corporate governance mechanisms should be used to address these issues. Indeed, in our discussion on how blockchain systems can be more effectively regulated and governed, we do use concepts and measures drawn from corporate governance, such as "regulation via governance" achieved through the shaping of social norms and incentives (chapter 8).

Yet, the lens of corporate governance alone is insufficient to understand the complexity of blockchain governance. First, the status of permissionless blockchains as a shared infrastructural technology—a common good—calls for insights from political science and political economy (e.g., commons management).[25] Second, though there are certainly applications of blockchain technology that may draw lessons from theories of corporate governance, there are several that do not fit the corporate mold, with ambitions ranging from rewilding the planet to creating new states. In other words, these systems involve participants who have motivations other than that of the competitive *homo economicus*. Consequently, some scholars have called for the design of blockchain governance institutions that are not primarily economically oriented.[26] Given this heterogeneity, concepts from political theory (and sociology) such as legitimacy, trust, and states of exception prove to be useful not only for understanding centralized, coercive political systems but also for shedding light on the distinct challenges and tensions faced by a wide range of decentralized, noncoercive blockchain-based systems. Third, many blockchain systems have intentionally embraced the language and practices of political governance—with participants engaging in group deliberation on forums, casting regular votes, drafting constitutions, and discussing concepts like legitimacy and alegality. This culture requires far more participatory involvement than that required of an individual shareholder of a typical public corporation.

While some of these reasons for studying blockchain governance might seem abstract at first, this book will show, by means of examples, that they have real consequences. Our selection of examples is based on a desire to illustrate the implications of different governance choices on the operations of blockchain systems with canonical cases, while also providing an account of more recent cases, which might eventually become landmark cases in the history of blockchain governance. For instance, the example of Steem (chapter 4) shows how a neglect of the role of trust in blockchain networks can lead to problematic centralized dynamics, including hostile takeovers. The DAO attack (chapter 5) illustrates how blockchain networks can suffer emergency crises, which might lead to violations of their core principles. The recent examples of Ooki DAO (chapter 3) and the Tornado Cash (chapter 6) show how even relatively simple blockchain applications can challenge the boundaries of legal systems, leading lawmakers to take drastic and sometimes draconian countermeasures. These concrete examples demonstrate the relevance of discussing blockchain governance in the light of legal and political theory, and hence the relevance of this book for blockchain developers, policymakers, and anyone with a general interest or stake in the technology.

This Book

Blockchain Governance places itself at the heart of a burgeoning global conversation between academics, developers, and policymakers. The book starts with an in-depth introduction to the technical aspects of blockchain and the particular governance forms it enables (chapter 2). From there, it embeds the discussion on blockchain governance within the broader context of Internet governance. It argues that blockchain technology has enabled a shift from the *rule by code* model of traditional Internet platforms to a new *rule of code* model, with particular implications for the interaction with traditional *rule of law* systems (chapter 3).

The book then investigates a concept central to the political and legal visions of blockchain, its purportedly "trustless" character (chapter 4). Responding to sociological work on trust, it argues that blockchain technology could best be understood as a "confidence machine" even though the need for trust is not eliminated but rather dispersed within a distributed network of actors. Drawing from the historical event of The DAO attack, the book subsequently turns to the question of sovereignty in blockchain systems (chapter 5). It argues that blockchain systems are organized as positivist legal orders and that, like the legal orders of nation-states, they are vulnerable to the states of exception that urge the emergence of sovereign decision-making.

Subsequently, the book investigates two avenues to further develop and expand thinking about blockchain governance. The first avenue is centered around the concept of alegality taken from legal philosophy (chapter 6), which implies that legal orders have distinct boundaries that can be transgressed. The book argues that blockchain technology sometimes transgresses the boundaries of existing legal orders. Although regulators still have the means to address these transgressions in many cases (e.g., through enforcement of existing law or amendments to the law), certain alegal acts put into question how a legal order draws the legal/illegal boundary. The second avenue addresses the pivotal political concept of "legitimacy" (chapter 7), which in recent years has also become a focal point in discussions about blockchain governance. The book lays out a comparative discourse, distinguishing between the concepts of social constitutionalism and digital constitutionalism and providing a new concept that has been referred to as "blockchain constitutionalism." It discusses several understandings of legitimacy in this context, ranging from a thin understanding of "legitimacy as legality" to a thicker understanding of legitimacy as including substantive concerns, such as human rights and environmental justice.

The book concludes by laying out possible futures for blockchain governance (chapter 8). In light of the potential fields of application of blockchain technology, it investigates possible legal or regulatory regimes that might be developed to support or suppress the technology as well as possible future configurations of blockchain governance.

As it draws to a close, it is our hope that the book will have persuaded the reader to think about the ways in which legal and political theory on the one hand, and blockchain governance on the other, can enrich one another. This might turn out to be of great importance, once the speculative blockchain hype dies out and the technology becomes part of the infrastructure of our everyday lives and politics.

BLOCKCHAIN

A specter is haunting the modern world, the specter of crypto-anarchy.

—Timothy May, *Crypto-Anarchist Manifesto*[1]

Cash for Eternity

"Who wants to live forever?" Queen's evocative song echoes through the centuries, for humans have always been obsessed with the prospect of immortality. Yet, the means at our disposal to achieve immortality have changed over time. In ancient civilizations, immortality could only be achieved by performing great deeds that would be remembered throughout history. This is the case, for instance, with Tutankhamun, Alexander the Great, and Qin Shi Huang, whose lives endure in the history books of modern societies. But this type of immortality does not satisfy everyone. Like the medieval alchemists, humans have long been searching for another form of immortality, more closely related to biological life. This type of immortality is not about being forever remembered but rather about extending biological life.

Hannah Arendt argued that our understanding of time and history is intimately connected with our scientific understanding of the universe: an immeasurable expanse of moving particles, indifferent to human affairs.[2] Today, we understand that entropy is a core feature of the universe, which constantly pushes toward diffusion and disorder. Yet, there is also "extropy" in the universe: forces that tend toward fusion and order. Life is the most eminent of these forces.

Hal Finney, an influential American software developer and cryptographer, pondered upon the prospects of immortality: "If you accept that it is possible in principle for medicine to give us an unlimited healthy lifespan, then all you really need to do is to live in a universe where that medical technology is discovered, and then avoid accidents."[3]

Finney described the "self" as a lucky arrangement of billions of atoms in the brain. Hence, according to him, immortality simply requires preserving the brain's hardwiring. In 2009, Finney was diagnosed with a deadly disease:

amyotrophic lateral sclerosis (ALS). Confronted with his imminent death in 2014, he underwent a medical procedure where his body was cryogenized at a low temperature to ensure preservation of the tissues. His hope was that if one day the tissues' physical conditions could be solved by medical science, they would be awakened so that they can continue living.

Finney was part of the extropian movement,[4] popularized in the 1980s by the philosopher Max More—an early advocate for cryogenics. In 1990, More published the "Extropian Principles"[5] to help people understand how technological advances could liberate humanity from its physiological limits, opening up new opportunities for never-ending progress. The subsequent publication of *Extropy: The Journal of Transhumanist Thought* brought together a small group of future-minded scientists, researchers, and engineers interested in exploring the use of new technologies, such as artificial intelligence (AI), robotics, nanotechnology, space exploration, and life extension, to "upgrade" humanity.

While cryogenics purported to preserve individual lives, extropians were also interested in sustaining a certain form of collective life. They believed that technological progress and innovation could only flourish in a free market environment, liberated from hierarchic control. As claimed by More, "societies with pervasive and coercively enforced centralized control cannot allow dissent and diversity," as "no group of experts can understand and control the endless complexity of an economy and society composed of other individuals like themselves."[6] Extropians regard governmental regulations as obstacles to the freedom to innovate, and taxes as a distortion of the free market's ability to effectively allocate resources. The saying goes that death and taxes are the two things you can't escape, yet that is precisely what the extropians were trying to do. To escape taxes requires moving away from governments and politics, indulging in experiments of "libertarian exit"[7] that might require moving into new territories—on earth or in space settlements.[8] To escape from death requires creating things that can persist for eternity, both in the physical and digital world, without the need for anyone to look after them. The development of a global and decentralized digital currency—the extropians believed—was key to achieving these goals.

These ideas were shared with an adjacent and somewhat overlapping movement: the *cypherpunks*—a loose group of anarchists, libertarians, cryptographers, and software developers interested in exploring the use of cryptography to protect individual privacy and online liberties. Like the extropians, the cypherpunks were fiercely antigovernment and regarded centralized institutions as the source of all worldly corruption. The prominent

The saying goes that death and taxes are the two things you can't escape, yet that is precisely what the extropians were trying to do.

cypherpunk Timothy C. May wrote in the *Crypto-Anarchist Manifesto*, back in 1989:

> A specter is haunting the modern world, the specter of crypto anarchy. Computer technology is on the verge of providing the ability for individuals and groups to communicate and interact with each other in a totally anonymous manner. Two persons may exchange messages, conduct business, and negotiate electronic contracts without ever knowing the true name, or legal identity, of the other. . . . Just as the technology of printing altered and reduced the power of medieval guilds and the social power structure, so too will cryptologic methods fundamentally alter the nature of corporations and of government interference in economic transactions.[9]

Thus, while the extropians looked for ways to extend life, the cypherpunks focused on letting go of governmental institutions or any other corruptible intermediary authority. Despite their different ambitions, both groups were concerned with improving individual and collective autonomy. What they had in common was the need for a shared record of accounts, an uncensorable, immutable, and immortal digital currency not controlled by any single individual or group and that could persist for generations, independently of any single institutional framework.[10]

Digital Cash

One of the first attempts at creating anonymous digital cash can be traced back to David Chaum, one of the most influential members of the cypherpunk movement. Chaum's doctoral dissertation explored the use of cryptography to create trusted networks of untrusted nodes. In 1989, he attempted to operationalize his theoretical insights through the development of a new digital currency system—which he called DigiCash—using cryptographic techniques to allow for anonymous and untraceable transactions. DigiCash came with many significant benefits for users interested in financial privacy and merchants interested in a secure way to engage in commercial transactions online. However, as opposed to today's cryptocurrencies, DigiCash required a central authority to act as a trusted intermediary for all electronic transactions. Chaum managed to enter into commercial partnerships with a few banks, but DigiCash failed to gain greater traction.

DigiCash enabled users to anonymously withdraw digital notes from their bank so that they could subsequently be exchanged off market, or directly send payments of any value to third parties. The project gained attention among the cypherpunk community, but governments and merchants were concerned about the anonymity it provided. Many banks saw it as a competitive product rather than as an opportunity to improve their services to their clients, and most consumers simply did not understand the need for digitally mediated transactions. As the project failed to gain more mainstream adoption, Chaum's company went bankrupt in 1998.

The cypherpunks were undeterred by this setback. Other attempts were made at creating decentralized digital cash. Wei Dai and Nick Szabo proposed alternative implementations of digital currencies (known as b-money and BitGold, respectively) using proof of computation (proof of work, PoW) to secure the issuance of new currency. Yet, both approaches suffered from the double-spending problem, enabling users to fool the network to spend the same money twice. Building upon these initial developments, in 2004, Hal Finney created an anonymous currency called RPOW, where users could only be identified through their cryptographic keys. However, like Chaum's DigiCash, RPOW also relied on a centralized system in charge of ensuring that no one could spend more money than they actually have. As such, it failed to fulfill the requirement of being completely autonomous and independent from any central authority.

While the cypherpunks were still working on the design of secure and anonymous digital cash, the world went through a period of great turmoil. The global financial system had expanded the range of new financial products, like collateralized debt obligations, whose collaterals had become increasingly risky. The whole edifice of globalized finance came tumbling down on September 15, 2008, when the large American investment bank Lehman Brothers filed for bankruptcy. This triggered a series of bailouts, as governments decided to inject billions of dollars of public money to prevent the collapse of the global financial system. This reinforced the convictions of the extropians and cypherpunks: centralized powers—be they banks or governments—could and should not be trusted. The cypherpunk revolution was about to be unleashed.

On October 31, 2008, Finney's attention was drawn to an email sent to the cypherpunk mailing list, by an anonymous contributor known as Satoshi Nakamoto. "I've been working on a new electronic cash system that's fully peer-to-peer, with no trusted third party," Nakamoto wrote, with a reference to a paper titled "Bitcoin: A Peer-to-Peer Electronic Cash System."[11] In this paper, Nakamoto outlined the specification for a new digital currency that would be powered by a network of computers rather than by a central authority. This system, which he called Bitcoin, leveraged previous work done by cryptographers and computer scientists like the aforementioned cypherpunks as well as Ron Rivest, Adi Shamir, and Leonard Adleman (RSA public-key cryptography), Hans Peter Luhn (hash functions), and Ralph Merkle (Merkle trees).

Bitcoin also built upon the work of physicist Scott Stornetta and cryptographer Stuart Haber, who—already in the 1990s—had devised a system relying on a network of dispersed but interconnected copies of a shared ledger in order to solve the problem of time stamping and authenticity in the digital realm. Their solution was to record data into a series of time-stamped digital "blocks," each referencing the "hash" (i.e., the digital digest) of the previous block so that altering information in one block would require altering all the blocks connected afterwards. They called this technology a "blockchain"—and they went on to create the first blockchain that ever existed.

Nakamoto combined all these primitives together with advanced peer-to-peer technologies, cryptography, and game theoretical incentives to generate a decentralized, secure, verifiable, and immutable ledger for financial transactions.[12]

A few months after Nakamoto's email, the ideas described within his white paper had been translated into software. Nakamoto launched the Bitcoin network on January 3, 2009, with the creation of the first genesis block, which generated the first set of Bitcoins allocated to Nakamato's address. Embedded within the first block was the headline of an article from *The Times* newspaper: "Chancellor on brink of second bailout for banks"—a message revealing the motivations behind the creation of Bitcoin while also providing proof regarding the network's launch date.

Today, Finney is known as the person who received the first Bitcoin transaction, on January 12, 2009. Perhaps more than anyone else, he immediately saw the great promise of Nakamoto's invention.

Over the years, Bitcoin gained increased popularity, and—despite its volatility—by 2011 there were already a few businesses accepting Bitcoin as a form of payment as well as a few organizations, like Wikileaks, accepting donations in Bitcoin. This is also the year in which Nakamoto retired from the Bitcoin project, and the community has since been led by a small number of core developers. With its ability to provide a global, decentralized, and censorship-resistant monetary system that operates outside of any governmental control, Bitcoin is an important step toward realizing the vision of both the cypherpunks and the extropians. Nakamoto's association with these groups suggests that they may have influenced the creation of Bitcoin. At the same time, while Nakamoto was an early adopter and supporter of both movements, there is no evidence that Satoshi is still active in either community.

The Technology

By cleverly combining existing innovations, Nakamoto's Bitcoin solved three problems all at once. First, it eliminated the need for a centralized issuing authority (the mint) by introducing a protocol of decentralized money issuance based on individual contributions to a peer-to-peer network

Client-Server   Peer-to-Peer

Figure 1   Client server architecture and peer-to-peer architecture.

(figure 1). Second, it solved the need of having a centralized authority to address the double-spending problem by
means of a decentralized ledger with a guaranteed, tamper-
resistant, and shared history of time-stamped transactions.
Third, it solved the security problem by means of an incen-
tivization system (PoW) that automatically increases the
security of the network as the network's value increases.
Simply put, Bitcoin combines the functionalities of a mint,
a bank, and a currency in one decentralized network.

Bitcoin's decentralized ledger comes with specific features that enable the establishment of a shared history
between all network nodes. The problem in most peer-
to-peer networks is that there is no agreed-upon notion
of time, making it impossible for network participants to
agree upon the order of messages they receive. To avoid
double spending, where the same transaction is sent to
two different users at the same time, Bitcoin introduces

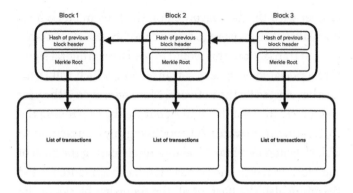

Figure 2 Diagram of a blockchain.

a mechanism to collectively keep track of the order of transactions by linking blocks one after the other. Every block of transactions is uniquely identified through its cryptographic hash (i.e., a digital fingerprint unique to that block)[13] and includes a reference to the hash of the previous block. This creates a long chain of blocks that chronologically reference each other, where the hash of every block is incorporated in the following block (figure 2).

The content of the Bitcoin blockchain can only be updated in an append-only manner, by adding information to it, but it cannot be retroactively altered or modified, at least in theory. The combination of cryptographic hashes and Merkle trees, along with other cryptographic primitives such as public-private key cryptography and digital signatures, makes it virtually impossible for anyone to tamper with the data recorded on the Bitcoin blockchain. If a malicious user were to try and modify the content of a Bitcoin transaction, this would invalidate the digital signature associated with such a transaction, which will therefore be rejected by the network. Moreover, even if the user could recreate a valid digital signature (by controlling the corresponding private key), modifying any transactions in a block would necessarily require recalculating the hash of the block in which the transaction has been stored—and therefore also the hash of all the following blocks in the chain, whose reference to the previous block would otherwise be broken. This makes blockchain-based applications particularly well suited for applications where data integrity is of paramount importance, such as in the case of financial transactions.

In practice, however, a malicious user could still modify a blockchain's history by recalculating the hashes of all the following blocks in the chain. While the exercise might be tedious, it could be potentially achieved with a limited amount of computational power. In Bitcoin, this problem is solved by means of the PoW algorithm. Nakamoto introduced a particular implementation of PoW, in which network participants compete to solve a cryptographic puzzle, whose difficulty is adjusted based on the amount of computational resources currently engaged in the network. Solving that puzzle is a precondition for anyone to be able to submit a new block to the network.

Hence, even though all network participants are responsible for verifying and validating transactions, only some of these participants—called miners—are also responsible for creating blocks of transactions (figure 3) that will be added to the Bitcoin blockchain. In order to propose a new block to the network, miners need to find the solution to a mathematical puzzle that requires an increasing amount of computational power, as the number of miners increases. The puzzle consists in finding a particular "nonce" to insert in the header of a block, in order to ensure that the resulting hash for that block is sufficiently small. The difficulty of this puzzle is determined by the Bitcoin protocol and evolves over time in order to ensure that a new block is added, on average, every ten minutes. If blocks are created too fast, the Bitcoin protocol will increase the difficulty of the puzzle; vice versa, if blocks take too long to be created, the Bitcoin protocol will automatically decrease the difficulty. Miners engage in this computational effort because the first one to solve the mathematical puzzle, and therefore to create a new block, is rewarded with a specified amount of Bitcoin (the block reward), as well as the transaction fees for all transactions included into the block, as a compensation for their efforts. This creates a race among miners, who are economically incentivized to expend significant amounts of computational power in order to be the first to find a new block.

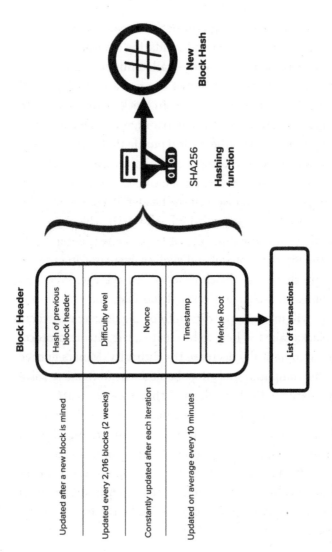

Figure 3 Diagram of a block of transactions.

As a consequence of these features, blockchain systems are described as being *technically distributed* across numerous nodes instead of centralized in servers controlled by a single operator. As all transactions are replicated and distributed across the network participants, there is no single point of failure, and consequently the network is resilient against attacks and censorship. Instead of an operator being able to unilaterally change software without the authorization of users, blockchain networks are noncoercive as participants must actively accept any proposed changes and can decide to fork a protocol rather than accept changes. Relatedly, as network nodes verify and validate all transactions submitted to the network, the existence of transactions is transparent and traceable. At the same time, despite this transparency of transactions, participants can engage with a network without using their real-world identities. In other words, these networks allow for pseudonymous participation.

Bitcoin is a new form of digital cash whose "production and transaction is constrained by expenditure" of computational energy.[14] PoW blockchains like Bitcoin are today heavily criticized for requiring significant electricity consumption for their operations.[15] This resource-intensive design is charged with contributing to global heating. Alternative consensus mechanisms have emerged over time, such as proof of stake (PoS), which greatly reduce the amount of computational resources expended in the block production process. In a PoS system, network participants are selected to add a new block to the blockchain based on the number of coins they have staked. This means that competition between validating nodes is no longer based on the amount of computational power invested into the network. Similarly, rewards for participation are not based on the amount of computation that each node has put in the network but rather on the relative share of tokens they have staked. Conversely, if these participants fail to maintain the blockchain, their stakes can be slashed. The Ethereum blockchain transitioned from PoW consensus to a PoS system to drastically reduce energy consumption, among other things.[16]

Finally, while Bitcoin is decentralized at the infrastructural level, it is not necessarily so at the operational level since it is difficult to know who ultimately controls the nodes in the network. Yet, the degree of decentralization of a blockchain network is crucial to its overall security and sustainability. Both PoW and PoS blockchains are vulnerable to the so-called 51 percent attack, where an attack to the network can be executed by a single entity controlling over 50 percent of the computational power (in the case of PoW) or over 50 percent of the overall stake in the network (in the case of PoS).

The rise of Bitcoin spurred the emergence of other blockchain-based networks like LiteCoin (2011), Name-Coin (2011), and, most notably, Ethereum (2014)—the brainchild of Vitalik Buterin. As the teenager editor of *Bitcoin Magazine*, one of the first publications dedicated to cryptocurrency and blockchain technology, Buterin realized that blockchain technology could be used not only as a ledger for cryptocurrency transactions but also as a means to deploy software code that could be used to automate these transactions. This opened up the possibility for any type of decentralized applications (DApps), even ones that could manage entire organizations of people.[17] The idea soon turned into a visionary project, which eventually became Ethereum.

Buterin designed Ethereum as the underlying infrastructure for a "world computer," where anyone could deploy code that could be used to power many different types of DApps. The particularity of Ethereum is that it features a built-in Turing-complete programming language allowing for code to be executed, in a distributed manner, by all nodes on the Ethereum blockchain.[18] As such, the Ethereum blockchain allows for the distributed execution of software code with a guarantee of execution of said code. Anyone can interact with these so-called *smart contracts* through a blockchain transaction that includes a series of "input" parameters. These parameters are processed by the smart contract's code according to a set of predefined conditions, generating an "output" that can trigger another transaction and ultimately alter the state of the blockchain.[19] Because every node in the network must obtain the exact same result from the smart contract's computation, smart contracts are always deterministic, meaning they can only execute in one specific manner, without the possibility of interference from a third party. Thus, once a smart contract is deployed on the Ethereum blockchain, its execution is guaranteed.

Ethereum's core idea is the closest implementation of what cypherpunk Nick Szabo had originally characterized as a "smart contract."[20] Smart contracts are not legal contracts in and of themselves, yet they enable people to enter into technologically driven contractual agreements with other people or machines. A large number of smart contracts exist on Ethereum today, allowing for a wide variety of applications to be carried out without the intervention of a centralized operator, such as executing payments or automating transactions, creating escrow accounts, or even creating decentralized finance (DeFi) platforms that are not operated by anyone but their own code. Most importantly for the purposes of this book, smart contracts can be leveraged to create so-called DAOs, allowing for people to pool resources together into a common treasury and collectively manage this treasury through a set of governance and decision-making procedures that have been enshrined into code and are therefore automatically enforced by the technological infrastructure of the underlying blockchain.

Ethereum first extended the functionality of Bitcoin beyond the cryptocurrency use case, and now many other blockchains have followed suit—including Hyperledger, Tezos, and Solana. Most of these blockchain systems, which are central to this book, are so-called public, permissionless blockchains. A public, permissionless blockchain is a decentralized, distributed ledger that is open to anyone. Public blockchains generally operate with pseudonymous identities, giving users means to preserve their (financial) privacy online. In contrast, so-called private blockchains are permissioned ledgers that are only accessible to approved participants. Participants are required to identify themselves in order to access and interact with private ledgers. The latter are generally adopted by large enterprises developing internal blockchain solutions to automate certain business processes. Enterprise blockchains are also being developed by consortia of companies in a wide range of industries, including finance, health care, supply chain management, and energy. Because most of the governance innovations are occurring in the context of public blockchains, this book focuses on them over private or enterprise blockchain systems.

Tools for Governance

Since the advent of Bitcoin, blockchain technology has been developed and used for a variety of applications beyond cryptocurrencies. While initially geared toward the creation of digital scarcity, blockchain technology has become a new institutional technology[21] that facilitates the recording of information for authentication and verification purposes, the automation of operations through the use of smart contracts and DApps, and the creation of new organizational structures.[22] It thus becomes clear why blockchain technology is often associated with the theme of governance, considering its potential role in the creation and distribution of scarce (digital) resources, the issuance of authoritative claims or attestations (e.g., property certificates), the execution of automated contracts, and the provision of new decision-making mechanisms.

Digital Scarcity

Blockchains enable the exchange of various digital assets in a peer-to-peer fashion. While people have been distributing digital files over peer-to-peer networks like BitTorrent for many years now, distributing digital files over the Internet network always and necessarily implies a reproduction of these files: if I send you a digital song over the Internet, I still retain my digital copy of the song. This is what has led economists to qualify the digital realm as nonrival, meaning that consumption of a digital file by one person does not preclude the consumption of the same digital file by another person. The technological guarantees of blockchain technology make it impossible for any given actor to reproduce blockchain-based digital assets. We can now talk about "digital scarcity" (as opposed to the "artificial scarcity" introduced by intellectual property) regarding all digital assets that subsist on a blockchain.[23]

These digital assets can assume a variety of functions. Cryptocurrencies, like Bitcoin or Ethereum, are necessary for the use of the underlying blockchain network. Bitcoins are needed to pay the transaction fees to use the Bitcoin network, and Ether is needed to pay for the cost of executing transactions on the Ethereum blockchain. These cryptocurrencies can also be traded for other cryptocurrencies or traditional fiat currencies on specialized exchanges. Exchanges can be either centralized, like Coinbase or Kraken, or decentralized, like Uniswap or Sushiswap.[24]

Blockchain tokens are another type of digital assets issued on a blockchain that represent a specific resource or utility. Today, there are a variety of different blockchain platforms used for the issuance of digital tokens. The most well-known is probably Ethereum, which supports the issuance and exchange of a wide variety of token-based digital assets. Most blockchain tokens provide the ability to access a certain service or use a certain blockchain application: these are usually referred to as utility tokens.[25]

Sometimes, tokens represent fractional ownership in a project or asset that has been tokenized on a blockchain. These are called security tokens and often resemble more traditional investments, like equity or debt. Oftentimes, these tokens are offered to the public by the means of token sales, also known as initial coin offerings (ICOs), used to raise funds to develop a particular blockchain-based initiative. Whether they refer to shares in a company or in a blockchain-based entity, the sale of these tokens is commonly assimilated to an investment contract, where the purchasers expect some financial return on their investment through the efforts of others. As a result, the issuance and trading of these tokens are generally highly regulated because they typically fall within the scope of securities regulations.

Some blockchain tokens are also associated with the possibility to participate in the governance of a particular blockchain system. By acquiring a token, one thus automatically acquires the possibility to cast a vote regarding a particular issue—and the more tokens one holds, the more influence one has in the decision-making process. Thus, as opposed to the democratic principle of "one person, one vote," blockchain systems typically implement a plutocratic governance system based on "one token, one vote," more akin to shareholder voting. This essentially means that those with more economic power have the possibility of swaying the decision-making process to their own advantage by purchasing more tokens. A variety of solutions have been elaborated to mitigate this problem. For instance, *quadratic voting*[26] allows people to express the intensity of their preferences by casting multiple votes on a single issue, with votes being discounted by a quadratic formula. As such, it provides individuals with a more granular means of expressing their preferences, granting more weight to deeply held convictions while nonetheless ensuring a fair representation of the opinion of the masses. In addition, as a complement or as an alternative to these forms of token-based voting, a variety of reputation-based governance systems have progressively been built and adopted by several blockchain systems,[27] relying on nontransferable tokens to implement more meritocratic governance systems.

Tokens can also be used to represent certificates of ownerships for physical assets (e.g., gold) or digital assets (e.g., works of art). The latter are usually referred to as NFTs (nonfungible tokens). NFTs are a type of digital asset that are unique and nonfungible (meaning they cannot be replaced by another identical asset) as they each have their own distinct value. For the first time in history, artists have the ability to monetize their digital artworks without having to transfer the copyright in these works, for what they are selling is not the intellectual property associated with the work but rather unique digital copies of that work. One of the most well-known NFTs is Beeple's "Everydays: The First 5,000 Days," which was sold for USD 69 million at a Christie's auction in March 2021. Following that sale, the NFT market has seen a boom in both the number of NFTs being created and the prices being paid for them. The digital scarcity inherent in these tokens has resulted in significant speculative dynamics in the NFT market, leading to an overall market capitalization of over USD 20 billion in 2022. And even though the speculative bubble has eventually burst, NFTs remain today a powerful means for the trading of (scarce) digital assets.

NFTs are also increasingly used to create new types of virtual communities, whose membership is defined by the ownership of NFTs from a particular collection. The Bored Ape Yacht Club is perhaps the most representative example of this trend. This NFT collection of 10,000 Bored Apes has become one of the most expensive and influential NFT projects due to its focus on community benefits. Every Bored Ape NFT is not only an expensive collectible but also a community pass, enabling token holders to access exclusive community meetups all over the world and hang out with other Bored Apes. As such, NFTs are also being turned into a governance tool, with the advent of token-gated communities or forums, where ownership of an NFT becomes a precondition to access a particular type of community's resources or even to engage with the governance of such a community.

Authentication
Blockchain technology provides new ways to verify and authenticate content as well as to gain secure and verifiable attestations or certifications. Instead of a digital

notary service, with a blockchain, the authenticity of digital documents can be verified by simply consulting the information recorded on the chain. This functionality has been used already for a variety of applications, including the issuance of university diplomas and birth certificates.

Indeed, while data recorded on a blockchain will remain forever accessible to all (at least as long as the blockchain network remains operative), it is also possible to record information on a blockchain through the use of hashes. This digital fingerprint constitutes an incorruptible proof that the file existed at that point in time in which the hash has been recorded on the blockchain and that the person initiating the transaction was most likely in possession of that file. The benefit of this approach is that no one accessing the blockchain will ever be able to retrieve the content of the information associated with the hash. Yet, anyone possessing the original file will be able to verify ex post that the file is authentic and its content has not been tampered with.

More recently, new modalities of certification or attestations have been brought forward in the blockchain space through the popularization of nontransferable tokens. These tokens are issued to a particular account by a recognized entity or peer in order to certify that the account holder fulfills specific requirements—whether such a system is used by a governmental authority to attest that someone is a US citizen or by a community member to declare that someone is a recognized member of a particular community. Because these tokens are nontransferable, they can be used to ensure that the account holder does indeed exhibit the relevant attributes or characteristics associated with those tokens. This opens a new window of opportunities for governance experimentation in blockchain-based systems that are not bound to a plutocratic tendency (where people can purchase tokens to acquire more voting power) but rather to a meritocratic tendency (where people have to earn tokens based on their attributes or skills, or according to their contributions to a particular initiative).

Ensuring the reliability and trustworthiness of blockchain-based attestations and certifications is not devoid of any challenges. While the blockchain eliminates the possibility of forging a certificate or tampering with a previously issued credential, it does not as such guarantee the accuracy of the information stored within—also known as the problem of *garbage in, garbage out*. To the extent that they relate to information off-chain, for these blockchain-based credentials to be recognized as legitimate, they must demonstrate a rigorous verification and validation process, ideally undertaken by a trusted actor. Trusted actors who act as intermediaries between the on- and off-chain world are usually referred to as *oracles*, recording real-world information into the blockchain so that such information becomes available to smart contracts and other blockchain-based applications to act upon. The more real-world information a blockchain system needs, the greater the influence of oracles in ensuring the proper operations of that system. Therefore, it is increasingly more important to ensure that these oracles provide accurate and reliable data.[28]

Decision-Making

The most advanced blockchains that support the deployment of smart contracts also make it possible to create more sophisticated technological arrangements, using software code to ensure that specific transactions are automatically executed whenever specific conditions are met. The traditional way to think about smart contracts is by analogy with a vending machine.[29] The analogy is useful in showing that a technological infrastructure (i.e., the vending machine) can guarantee that a particular contract (with the vendor) will be fulfilled as intended, with no possibility of breach—unless one were to tamper with the vending machine. Hence, this interaction requires no trust among the contracting parties: the vending machine has no choice but to deliver the goods upon receiving the money. Yet, the analogy falters because unlike a vending machine that can easily be destroyed or tampered with (if the amount in the machine is greater than the cost of breaking it), the technological guarantees of blockchain technology make it virtually impossible to stop or influence the execution of a smart contract, unless the code specifically provides for it.[30]

The programmability of blockchains and associated smart contracts enabled the creation of so-called DApps, which are pieces of software running on a blockchain that anyone can transact with. The use of DApps has also been proposed, more explicitly, as a way to create new organizational structures enabling people to coordinate themselves through a set of self-executing rules deployed on a blockchain. These are usually referred to as DAOs.[31] Despite the name, a DAO is not fully autonomous. Rather, a DAO is an organization that is collectively managed by a community of members through a set of technical rules encoded in a smart contract, with no need for any centralized authority or administrative board.[32] Accordingly, DAOs allow for the experimentation and implementation of more distributed and bottom-up governance systems. Indeed, because they have no management structure or CEO, DAOs necessarily require the intervention of their members to interact with their smart contracts to implement decision-making rules.

There are many types of DAOs, which can fulfill different functions: from the management of a common treasury among people who do not necessarily know or trust each other, to operating a crowdfunding or investment platform where contributors are granted with a governance right over the project they contributed to, to administering an organization of people with a codified decision-making apparatus and a more decentralized governance structure.[33]

There are now several successful DAOs: Moloch DAO, for decentralized investments in blockchain infrastructure; Decentraland DAO, operating a decentralized planning committee in the metaverse; Mirror DAO, running the curation for a decentralized blogging platform; Lex DAO, gathering a group of legally minded engineers providing services for other DAOs; and the Friends with Benefits DAO, operating a members-only social club for crypto enthusiasts. There are even a few projects that see DAOs as an opportunity to create new self-sovereign structures that could effectively bypass or replace nation-states, thereby creating new "blockchain-based virtual nations"[34] or "network states."[35] These communities of kinship leverage blockchain technology to self-organize through their own cryptocurrency, blockchain-based census system, and technologically driven governance structure, based on the principles of voluntary association.

* * *

After having outlined the development of blockchain technology as it evolved from a platform for digital cash to a more general purpose technology, chapter 2 has shown how its distinctive features—such as decentralization, immutability, pseudonymity, and verifiability—have enabled the emergence of new DApps with their own governance models, culminating in the advent of DAOs: decentralized organizations that operate in a distributed manner through collective governance. These emergent technologies present both challenges and opportunities in the field of governance. On the one hand, they offer the promise of enhanced transparency, trust, and efficiency in various sectors, from finance to supply chain management. On the other hand, they introduce novel complexities related to legal frameworks, security vulnerabilities, and decision-making processes that require careful examination and innovative solutions. In the chapters that follow, we delve deeper into the multifaceted landscape of blockchain-based governance, exploring the intricacies, successes, and ongoing debates in this rapidly evolving field.

RULE OF CODE

On behalf of the future, I ask you of the past to leave us alone. You are not welcome among us. You have no sovereignty where we gather.

—John Perry Barlow, *Declaration of the Independence of Cyberspace*[1]

Runaround

On a distant planet, in a faraway corner of the galaxy, a lone robot is laboring away in an environment that is lethal for humans. Its mission is to collect a rare mineral, selenium, which is crucial for the sustenance of the operations on the planet. Speedy, like many other robots of its kind, has been programmed to abide by the Three Laws of Robotics. These laws stipulate that a robot (1) may not injure a human being, (2) must obey orders given by human beings except where such orders would conflict with the first law, and (3) must protect its own existence as long as such protection does not conflict with the first or second laws.

In Asimov's *I, Robot* stories, these three laws are intended as a safety measure to prevent robots from harming humans. Yet, as the story illustrates, although they are apparently consistent, these three laws could, in some rare circumstances, lead to unexpected and seemingly incoherent behaviors. Indeed, as Speedy realizes that the source of selenium can cause harm to its electromechanical structure (thus threatening its own existence), and that preservation of its electromechanical structure is a requirement to fulfill its mission (thus obeying human orders), Speedy gets stuck in a circular logic loop and begins to act erratically, ultimately endangering the mission and the humans involved.

Written in 1941, Speedy's story highlights the potential dangers of relying too heavily on AI without fully understanding how it works or being able to fully predict its behavior. Most importantly, it illustrates how—regardless of the robot's actual intentions—any attempt at regulating AI systems with human laws will always lead to confusion due to the inherent ambiguity and flexibility of natural language.

When combined with a blockchain-based infrastructure, these challenges become even more problematic. Even if they do not come with sophisticated AI (yet), blockchain-based systems have already been deployed, operating autonomously on a distributed ledger, independently of any centralized authority. By virtue of their technical characteristics, these systems can be created in such a way that no one has the power to shut them down (i.e., there is no kill switch). They will continue to operate as long as there are enough nodes maintaining the underlying blockchain on which they run. As we will see later in the chapter, some of these systems have already proven to be capable of harm, most notably financial harm, money laundering, and terrorism financing.

While it may be difficult to codify the laws of robotics into blockchain systems, which are incapable of comprehending human language, the alternative is to codify human laws into the strict and formal language of code. Yet, what computer code provides in terms of accuracy and precision, it loses in terms of flexibility and granularity. As such, it cannot adequately capture the nuances of human values, ethical principles, and morality that can only be expressed in natural language. Hence the paradox arises: on the one hand, blockchain-based systems cannot be expected to abide by the rule of law, which is formulated as general principles rather than specific instructions codified into code; on the other hand, any attempt at codifying Asimov's laws into the rule of code, with specific instructions based on if-then conditionals, will necessarily reduce them to a form that is too simplistic to be sufficiently meaningful.

Rule by Code

"Governments of the Industrial World, you weary giants of flesh and steel, I come from Cyberspace, the new home of Mind." Thus begins the Declaration of Independence of Cyberspace, written in 1996 by American author and political activist John Perry Barlow. Barlow continues: "You are not welcome among us. You have no sovereignty where we gather. . . . You have no moral right to rule us nor do you possess any methods of enforcement we have true reason to fear." Barlow regarded cyberspace as a place where individual sovereignty is neither derived from nor subordinate to the sovereignty of any state. Indeed, he believed that governments simply did not have the right, nor the effective capacity to, control this new world, saying "cyberspace does not lie within your borders."[2]

Barlow saw the Internet as an infrastructure governed by a set of protocols and standards (e.g., TCP/IP, HTTP, SMTP) encoded in the software and hardware layers of the network. Initially developed by the Defense Advanced Research Projects Agency, many of these protocols were subsequently developed through an open and decentralized process, thanks to the voluntary efforts of developers, researchers, and engineers—and later standardized by nonprofit organizations such as the Internet Engineering Task Force or the World Wide Web Consortium. This process of open-source development and standardization allowed for rapid and permissionless innovation, where anyone with a computer and an Internet connection can develop and deploy new applications without having to seek authorization from anyone.

Yet, Barlow's vision of a new digital space that escapes from governmental control failed to anticipate the role that code could play in governing the digital realm. He did not foresee that this new independent space could easily be co-opted by a new set of (private) actors, eager to establish their own (technical) rules into the digital domain.

The concentration of traffic in the hands of a few large online operators—chokepoints—is a threat to the open and decentralized nature of the Internet as originally envisioned by Barlow. Indeed, as companies like Google and Meta have grown in size and power, they have also come to exercise an increasingly large degree of control over the way we use the Internet. They have done this in a number of ways, including through the development of proprietary software and platforms that are not compatible with each other, through the use of algorithms that favor their own products and services over those of their competitors, and through the use of terms of service that give them the right to censor or delete content that they deem to be objectionable. Most importantly, these companies are leveraging code to precisely stipulate what users can or cannot do on their own platform, in ways that often go

Barlow's vision of a new digital space that escapes from governmental control failed to anticipate the role that code could play in governing the digital realm.

beyond[3]—and sometimes even contravene[4]—the laws of national jurisdictions.

In his book *Code and Other Laws of Cyberspace*, Lawrence Lessig analyzed the various ways in which the architecture of the Internet—including both the software and hardware layers—can shape and govern our behaviors in the digital space.[5] Drawing from his previous analysis of the four regulatory levers that can affect individual behaviors—law, market dynamics, social norms, and architecture (figure 4)—he concluded that on the Internet, architecture (or "code") had become the predominant mechanism to regulate online behaviors—which he described as "code is law."[6]

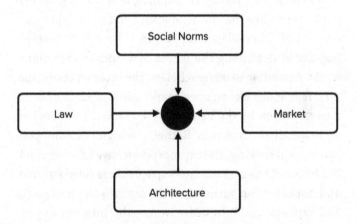

Figure 4 Lessig's four modes of regulation.

In recent years, the development of the Internet has become increasingly dominated by a small number of large companies, which control large parts of the Internet infrastructure. These include the servers that host our data (e.g., Amazon), the social media platforms that connect us (e.g., Facebook/Meta), the web browsers that we use and the operating systems that run our devices (e.g., Google/Android)—in addition to all the applications that we use to access our email, browse the web, use social media, and shop online. As a result, these online operators dictate what can or cannot be *technically done* on their platforms, independently of what can or cannot be *legally done*.

This has led to the emergence of cloud empires[7] with new functional sovereigns[8] reigning over our digital fiefdoms. Terms like "techno-feudalism"[9] and the neighboring concept of "surveillance capitalism"[10] have now become popular in describing the power dynamics in the online world. According to many scholars, the Internet landscape no longer looks like an open marketplace of ideas or even a space driven by the logics of free market, competition, and capitalistic dynamics. Rather, the logics of monopolization, rent seeking, and expropriation have taken ground. The Internet has evolved into a space that is ruled by "rent and dispossession, rather than the capitalist logic of profit and exploitation."[11] In order words, the Internet has become a space where capitalism has progressively given way to feudalism.

This new form of sovereignty presents a challenge to traditional forms of governance, as the rules that govern digital platforms are not always transparent or accountable to their "citizens."[12] Many democracies around the world operate according to the rule of law,[13] which prescribes—among other things—the principle of equality before the law (*nemo est supra legis*, or "no one is above the law"). In principle, laws are supposed to be applied equally to all citizens, and the government is subject to the same laws as the citizens. This ensures that individuals have certain rights and protections and the government operates within legal boundaries. This also means that laws and regulations can only be enacted and enforced according to specific rules that are subject to a variety of formal, procedural, and substantive constraints.

Conversely, some countries—mostly those under authoritarian regimes—operate according to the "rule by law."[14] In this context, laws are used to legitimize the actions of those in power rather than to protect the rights of citizens. Hence, the government is not necessarily subject to the same laws as the citizens, and laws may be selectively enforced or created to serve the interests of those in power. Because it prioritizes the government's authority over the rights and freedoms of the individual, the rule by law can easily lead to abuses of power and corruption.

When it comes to the regulation of Internet platforms, online operators generally have full discretionary power over the rules they chose to codify into their platforms, often with no accountability to any external authority nor any checks and balances. We introduce the concept of the "rule by code" to describe the governance of these online platforms: a regime where online operators have the power (and the tendency) to design and amend the code and technological infrastructure of their online platforms, primarily as a means to serve their own economic or political interests. The rule by code, characterized by the instrumentalization of computer code to serve the interests of powerful tech companies, thus presents itself as the software equivalent of the rule by law, characterized by the arbitrary wielding of laws to serve the interests of powerful sovereigns.

But the rule by code is not only instrumental to the interests of online operators. It can also serve the interest of governmental actors, insofar as the online operators that control the code are themselves under the jurisdiction of a sovereign authority. Indeed, many of the online platforms that are ruled by code can be (and have been) co-opted by established powers to serve their own political interests—as clearly shown by the successful efforts of US security services to collect data from large online platform operators at the expense of user privacy.[15] As Lawrence Lessig had foreseen, the technological infrastructure of centralized online platforms can be instrumentalized as a means to further the interests of both private operators and the political sovereign that regulates them. Hence, if it is true that governments may have a hard time regulating the behaviors of Internet users through traditional legal means, it is also true that governments retain the power to regulate the operators of online platforms within their own jurisdiction, requiring them to encode specific rules into their technical platforms to indirectly regulate the users of these platforms.

Despite the promises of early Internet advocates, today's Internet is not free from governmental control. It is heavily regulated through a set of laws and regulations that are imposed by nation-states upon centralized intermediaries and online operators. These include, among others, the European Union's Information Society Directive and the General Data Protection Regulation (GDPR), the US Digital Millennium Copyright Act, and the Children's Online Privacy Protection Act as well as more draconian measures such as the Chinese government's Great Firewall for the censorship of online content. All these measures are intended to regulate how online businesses can collect and use personal data, what their responsibilities are with regard to the content they host, and what type of content is accessible in each country. Sometimes, this plethora of regulations may lead to conflicting legal obligations across jurisdictions (e.g., copyright protection versus freedom of expression).

Rule of Code

We introduce the notion of the rule of code—by analogy to the rule of law—to illustrate how the core features of blockchain technology provide a set of fundamental features for blockchain-based networks and applications that distinguish them from traditional online applications (ruled by code) by inheriting some of the characteristics of the rule of law (in terms of traceability, verifiability, predictability, and accountability). While both traditional online platforms and blockchain-based systems rely on code to regulate online behaviors, there is nonetheless a fundamental difference in the way these two systems operate. Because there is no centralized authority controlling a public and permissionless blockchain network (i.e., there is no sovereign), blockchain technology provides for the establishment of code-based rules that are difficult to co-opt for the benefits of a few. The operations of these networks therefore require a much more distributed and polycentric governance system, where a multiplicity of actors need to agree (through distributed consensus) toward a particular course of action. This stands in contrast to the Internet governance discussions of the early 2000s, which were largely focused on centralized institutions or online operators and the need to trust them.

One of the most revolutionary aspects of blockchain technology—which is the most apparent in the context of public and permissionless blockchain networks—is its polycentric character. According to McGinnis,[16] polycentric systems consist of (1) multiple centers of decision-making authority with overlapping jurisdictions, (2) which interact through a process of mutual adjustment, (3) in order to generate a regularized pattern of overarching social order. Blockchain systems have the capacity to satisfy all three of these criteria.

The governance of public and permissionless blockchain networks is subject to multiple centers of decision-making, both endogenous and exogenous to the network. Examples of endogenous decision-making centers in the Ethereum ecosystem are full nodes (including validator nodes), staking pools, ETH holders, maximum extractable value (MEV) searchers, Ethereum core developers, Ethereum founders, and the Ethereum Foundation. Examples of exogenous decision-making centers are crypto exchanges, competing blockchain networks (e.g., Tezos, Cosmos, Cardano, EOS), regulatory bodies, policymakers, regulators, and a variety of entrepreneurs interfacing with the Ethereum network.[17] There are also overlapping functions among both endogenous and exogenous decision-making centers, with the Ethereum founders and Ethereum core developers, for instance, having overlapping authority over the future roadmap of Ethereum.

These multiple decision-making centers are in a constant process of interaction and mutual adjustment. For instance, Ethereum core developers and Ethereum nodes interact with one another whenever an upgrade is proposed for the network, as the latter are responsible for updating their clients to implement the upgrade. At the same time, the process of updating these clients can affect the planned development and roadmap of the Ethereum network. Similarly, companies that operate crypto exchanges are affected by laws and regulations that permit or restrict their activities, while the growing adoption and demand for cryptocurrencies, as indicated by growing crypto-exchange usage, can lead to changes in the relevant legislation. These endogenous and exogenous centers of decision-making also interact with one another across the edges of the network. For example, sanctions by state authorities on a series of smart contract addresses have caused some validators to censor transactions interacting with those addresses. At the same time, the actions and behavior of core developers can shape the perceptions of regulatory bodies and policymakers about the ability of developers to unilaterally change aspects of the protocol.

Finally, when it comes to the last criterion, blockchain protocols and their consensus algorithms stipulate a set of rules that all members of the network must abide by. The public nature of these on-chain rules provides a considerable degree of transparency about outcomes and helps ensure that incentives and rules align. In addition to the rules encoded directly in the protocol of a blockchain (on-chain), there also exists an overarching system of norms outlining the role of different decision-making centers with regard to the procedures and rules that must be followed to perform an operation off-chain, as for the various Bitcoin or Ethereum Improvement Proposals (BIPs and EIPs). Moreover, it often happens that the repeated patterns of interaction among multiple stakeholders give expression to a number of overarching norms and principles that most network participants abide by, such as the aspiration of immutability, irreversibility, and credible neutrality.

Looking at blockchain networks as polycentric governance systems helps us shed light on the fact that these networks operate according to a specific set of rules, where both the definition and the execution of these rules is not subject to the whims of any single actor but rather emerge from a multiplicity of interdependent agents exerting influence on the system. As Aligica and Tarko explain, polycentric systems are "rule of law systems" as power is not centralized in the hands of a single actor and agents are constrained by the rule of law.[18]

In sum, the *rule of law* refers to a system for governing human behavior whereby the laws are written down and applied equally to everyone, including the sovereign who remains accountable under the law.[19] It stands in contrast to the *rule by law*, where rules are applied arbitrarily and unevenly, at the sovereign's discretion. By analogy, the *rule of code* refers to a system for governing human behavior that is based on a series of code-based rules that apply equally to everyone regardless of their identity or role. As such, the rule of code stands in contrast to the arbitrary application of the *rule by code* by ensuring that no sovereign is above the code. This suggests that we may no longer need to trust the intentions of online operators as long as we have confidence in the operations of the code underpinning these new code-based applications.[20]

The notion of the rule of code was first introduced in 2018 by De Filippi and Wright in their book *Blockchain and the Law*. It has acquired new prominence in recent years with the progressive rise in popularity of blockchain technology. One key implication of the rule of code, as opposed to the rule by code, is that it removes the need for trust in centralized institutions or online intermediaries who rule over the code. In a world governed by the rule of code, the code rules in place of the sovereign—just as in the rule of law, the law ultimately rules over the sovereign. No government can interfere with a blockchain-based system, and no corporation can arbitrarily modify the code of a blockchain application because no one has the power to unilaterally modify the rules by which these systems operate—at least in theory.

The rules are encoded in the code itself, and everyone is subject to the same rules. Yet, this is not to say that the rule of code cannot be changed. The point is not for the rule of code to be immutable but rather for it to only be changeable in specific circumstances, in a decentralized and transparent way. That is, anyone can propose a change to the code, and the community can vote on whether to implement the change. This is similar to the way that laws are supposed to be amended under the rule of law.

Early blockchain advocates believed that the supremacy of code in blockchain-based systems would leave human inefficiencies and corruption behind.[21] They imagined a world where everyone would be bound by the same rules, accepted collectively by the community and enforced automatically by the underlying technological infrastructure, regardless of the identity or roles of the people concerned. As it turned out, this vision didn't come to life. Despite the technical issues and security flaws that some blockchain-based systems have witnessed over the years, the biggest challenge they encounter today is related to their governance structures.[22] One cannot assume that any blockchain application, by the mere fact of running on top of a blockchain, implements the rule of code. Indeed, it is often unclear who ultimately makes decisions about a project's development and what kind of participation or decision-making power have been granted to the various stakeholders. The governance of many existing blockchain applications is often highly centralized, either because the smart contract is controlled by a few actors through a multisignature wallet or because the governance tokens are concentrated in the hands of a few individuals.[23]

Moreover, while blockchain-based networks and applications are more likely to abide by the *rule of code*, there are many applications that interface with one or more blockchain systems while nonetheless abiding by the *rule by code*. This is the case, for instance, of many cryptocurrency exchanges, like Coinbase, Kraken, Binance, or the now infamous FTX, which are intended to facilitate the trading of various digital assets. Despite interfacing with a blockchain, these platforms are no different from traditional centralized online platforms: they are operated by companies incorporated in a particular jurisdiction and are therefore bound by the rules of that jurisdiction.

The recent legal actions by the US Securities and Exchange Commission (SEC) and the Commodity Futures Trading Commission (CFTC) against Coinbase and Binance highlight the regulatory challenges that centralized crypto exchanges face in the United States. The claim is that these exchanges have not only listed cryptocurrencies and tokens that the SEC believes are securities but have also operated as unregistered brokers.

Similarly, in Europe, the European Parliament and Council of the European Union recently passed the Markets in Crypto-Assets (MiCA) regulation,[24] extending jurisdiction to a variety of services not previously addressed by existing European financial regulations. The MiCA regulation applies to specific crypto assets (including commodity-backed or currency-backed stablecoins, e-money tokens, and other utility tokens but not NFTs) and associated issuers or service providers (such as custodial wallets, cryptocurrency exchanges, and crypto-portfolio management agencies). Under MiCA, crypto-asset providers are required to furnish comprehensive information concerning the crypto assets they issue, while adhering to disclosure and transparency rules. Meanwhile, crypto-asset service providers must undergo registration and enforce security protocols while adhering to antimoney laundering (AML) provisions. Yet, the MiCA regulation explicitly stipulates that it does not apply to all blockchain-based financial services that are provided in a "fully decentralized manner" and "without any intermediaries."[25] While it is currently unclear what may or may not qualify as "full decentralization," this provision effectively excludes (at least a portion of) what is generally referred to as DeFi from its scope.

Accordingly, legal liability becomes an important reason for favoring the *rule of code* over the *rule by code* when designing a blockchain-based system. Under the rule by code, whoever has the power to control the system's execution will also be held responsible for the outcome of such execution. Conversely, under the rule of code, the blockchain network itself is the authority that controls the system's execution and all the operations that occur within that system. The network participants are the users or, at best, the maintainers of the system and therefore cannot be held individually liable for the outcome of such operations. While some have argued[26] that the developers or designers of a blockchain-based systems are responsible for ensuring that the system is secure and operates as expected, such claim was refuted in a recent legal judgment[27] (under appeal at the time of writing). The judgment held that blockchain-based systems are developed by a fluctuating group of developers, many of whom are anonymous, and assigning liability to any of them would create an excessive burden on these few blockchain developers who can actually be identified. However, as discussed below, even under the rule of code, blockchain developers are not exempt from liability risks altogether as governments have already found ways to incriminate developers based on alternative grounds.[28]

Given the potential liability affecting many blockchain-based applications, there has been a progressive shift toward decentralizing blockchain projects that were originally implemented with a relatively centralized governance structure (rule by code) and progressively evolved into a DAO (rule of code). This process of "progressive decentralization"[29] has been put into practice, for instance, by Gitcoin (created in 2017 but only introducing a governance token in 2021) and MakerDAO (a stablecoin project operated at first via a foundation, which successfully engaged into a process of progressive decentralization in order to grow into a full-fledged DAO). All these initiatives can now be said to be governed by the rule of code in that there is no single actor (or group of actors) who can control or influence their operations, in a discretionary and unilateral manner.

Legal Tensions

While the rule of code presents a variety of benefits in terms of governance and resilience, when it comes to compliance with the law, there is a fundamental tension between the rule of code and the rule of law.[30] Indeed, because of the inherent properties of blockchain code, which is unambiguous and deterministic, the rule of code does not (and cannot) operate according to the same principles as the rule of law.

This is particularly visible in the context of property and contract law. Property is defined by law and can therefore also be taken away by the law. This means that anyone who acquires a particular asset in a way that is deemed to be illegitimate by the law will not be regarded as the legal owner of that asset and could potentially get it taken away by a court order. Conversely, in the context of blockchain-based assets, like cryptocurrencies or tokens, ownership is defined by the code of the blockchain-based system, and regardless of what the law says, no one has the power to seize these assets unless the code specifically provides for such a possibility. Similarly, in the context of contracts, legal contracts must be enforced by a third-party authority following the interpretation of the contractual terms in light of the provisions of contract law. In contrast, the code of a smart contract is automatically executed by the underlying blockchain infrastructure in a deterministic manner. This execution occurs regardless of whether the code properly reflects the parties' intentions or is compatible with the provisions of contract law.

This discrepancy with existing legal rules may be leveraged deliberately by some actors, purposely deploying blockchain-based applications to evade existing regulations (e.g., taxation and securities laws). Given that in the context of a permissionless blockchain network, or in the case of a decentralized blockchain-based application or DAO, no centralized entity can be held accountable for the activities undertaken on these blockchain-based systems, it becomes difficult to impute liability for any illicit act achieved through or via these systems. In other words, if the offender is not a legal entity but an actual piece of smart contract code, who should be held accountable for the offense?

As opposed to other technologies that can be more easily shut down by governmental authorities, it is relatively harder to effectively sanction blockchain-based systems (except in some rare situations, as described in the following section)—although those who publish or interact with the code might be incriminated. Because all transactions on a blockchain are recorded on a public ledger, these transactions can be traced back to the digital addresses of the participants in the network. Consequently, when an illicit transaction is made on a blockchain network, the transaction is visible on the public ledger, and the pseudonymous identity of the participant who made the transaction is also recorded. In principle, this could be used to trace an offender's real-world identity. In practice, however, it is very difficult to trace the identity of an offender in a blockchain network due to the pseudonymous nature of digital addresses. This challenge did not prevent regulators from enforcing the law in an emerging battle for supremacy between the rule of code and the rule of law.[31]

Take the infamous case of Silk Road, which was a dark web marketplace that was used to buy and sell illegal drugs and other illegal items. The marketplace was only accessible through the Tor network, a network that allows users to remain anonymous. Silk Road's payment system was operated via the pseudonymous Bitcoin blockchain. Hence, Silk Road users could buy and sell illegal items without revealing their real-world identities.

In 2013, the FBI shut down Silk Road and arrested Ross Ulbricht, the individual operating under the pseudonym "Dread Pirate Roberts." Despite the pseudonymous nature of the Bitcoin blockchain used for transactions on the site, it is not completely anonymous. This allowed the FBI to analyze the blockchain and link the digital addresses used by Dread Pirate Roberts to Ulbricht's identity.

Silk Road demonstrates that blockchain-based systems are not immune to law enforcement agencies. Although it can be very difficult to trace the real-world identity of a blockchain user, it is not impossible. In addition, it is important to note that the FBI was only able to arrest Ross Ulbricht because Silk Road was not a truly decentralized marketplace. Although it was using the Bitcoin blockchain for payments, it was not fully decentralized in its operation. As the operator of Silk Road, Pirate Robert was thus held responsible for the illicit activities that were undertaken onto the platform.

Another example of legal enforcement over a blockchain-based system is the case of Ooki DAO. The CFTC filed a complaint against the operations of Ooki DAO,[32] which was allegedly in violation of the Commodity Exchange Act by allowing users to engage in retail commodity derivative trading transactions without registering as a trading platform. The court held that although Ooki DAO had not been incorporated into a legal entity, it could be regarded as a general partnership or unincorporated association because it was "formed by mutual consent for the purpose of promoting a common objective" and could therefore be sued. To the extent that token holders could vote to promote the common objective of governing the Ooki protocol, ownership of governance tokens can result in DAO members being considered co-administrators or general partners of the DAO. This means that all members of the DAO are legally responsible for any actions taken by the DAO, and since there is no limited liability protection, the collective liability of the DAO becomes the individual liability of each member.

Yet, while all members of an unincorporated association are typically jointly and severally liable, in the case of Ooki DAO, given that many token holders were not active participants in the DAO, the court considered that liability would only be imputed to token holders who effectively exercised the governance rights associated with these tokens. Using their tokens to influence the activities of the DAO means that they are voluntarily becoming a member of the unincorporated association that governs the Ooki protocol. As a result, even though only the founders were held responsible for violating laws in the Ooki DAO case, the case suggests that in the future, all active token holders of a DAO could be held personally accountable for any illegal actions taken by the DAO, not just the founders. Because of these measures, anyone who interacts with the smart contract addresses will be held strictly liable, meaning there is no need to prove ill-intention or even awareness of the sanctions.

* * *

By revisiting the core properties of blockchain technology described in the previous chapters, chapter 3 focused on assessing their compatibility with established legal principles rooted in the rule of law. On the one hand, the chapter discussed how blockchain-based systems endeavor to emulate certain aspects of the rule of law by introducing what we refer to as the *rule of code*, made of predefined, automated, and transparent rules encoded directly into the technological fabric. This represents a fundamental shift from the more traditional *rule by code* of centralized online platforms as it guarantees that the code applies equally to everyone and no one stands "above the code." On the other hand, the chapter has shed light on some of the inherent limitations of this emerging paradigm of code-driven regulation, which might potentially come into conflict with existing regulatory frameworks. The insights from this chapter will inform the regulatory strategies and discussion in chapters 6 and 7.

PROBLEM OF TRUST

Oh, you have trusted somebody? Glad to hear of any instance of that sort. Reflects well upon all men.

—Herman Melville, *The Confidence Man*[1]

Con Men

On a day in April, in nineteenth-century America, a stranger boards a boat traveling along the Mississippi. Unbeknownst to his fellow passengers, he is a "confidence man." He plays psychological tricks on them, gaining their confidence to have a personal advantage. This central premise of Herman Melville's novel *The Confidence Man* popularized an infamous figure in American society. The confidence man (commonly abbreviated as "con man"),[2] according to Melville, is a stranger "in the extremest sense of the word."[3] A stranger, following sociologist Georg Simmel,[4] is a figure who unites nearness and remoteness, elements found in every human relationship; being physically close, part of a group (like the stranger on the boat), but in all other aspects "far," unknown, unfamiliar. The interesting thing about strangers is that we sometimes confide our most intimate thoughts to them because they lack the subjectivity and prejudice of the people near to us, who are part of our community of belonging.

America in the mid-nineteenth century was a special place because it was an eminent example of a society of strangers. People came from everywhere, from all backgrounds. Especially in sprawling metropolises like New York City, no one could be fully trusted outside of one's close-knit community because the place lacked what Simmel calls "organic" connections, built on shared histories and rituals of small communities or friends and family ties. Instead, America had to rely on "inorganic" connections: a shared language (English), monetary system (the dollar), civic education, and a set of social etiquettes. Many of these connections are mediated via sociotechnical systems, involving the interaction of social and technical components and subsystems. They also include things like credit reporting, which established a common, if very biased, measure of moral character.[5] These inorganic connections provide a common basis to confide in strangers. A confidence man is trained in exploiting these commonalities, relying on social systems like fashion and etiquette to appear respectable, kind, and reasonable—a model citizen.

The protagonist of *The Confidence Man* was, in all likelihood, modeled on a swindler named Thompson, who had been apprehended in New York City in 1849. He was found in possession of a great number of stolen watches that he had obtained from random strangers. One day later, his arrest was mentioned in the *New York Herald*: "For the last few months a man has been traveling about the city, known as the 'Confidence Man'; that is, he would go up to a perfect stranger in the street, and being a man of genteel appearance, would easily command an interview. Upon this interview he would say, after some little conversation, 'have you confidence in me to trust me with your watch until tomorrow.'"[6]

Three days later, the newspaper opened with a new piece. It wrote that the idea of the confidence man has to be extended beyond that of the individual swindler, for there are also confidence men of merchandise and politics. The real confidence men, the *Herald* claimed, are the people high up in the palaces of society: the bankers, the politicians, the financiers. The real "confidence man" is the one who lives and works on Wall Street.[7]

More than 150 years later, Satoshi Nakamoto had a similar epiphany. He lamented the "trust-based model" underlying the financial system, whose credibility had

The real "confidence man" is the one who lives and works on Wall Street.

eroded in the wake of the 2008 financial crisis. Like the swindler Thompson, the bankers had exploited people's confidence, albeit not in systems of etiquette and fashion but in the financial system. What had seemed to be an "objective" system that people took for granted with an unquestioning attitude had suddenly become highly questionable. People realized that without noticing it, they had confided in the banking sector as a third party that would take care of their finances. Contrary to the public's expectation, investment bankers had engaged in mind-blowing swindling, selling garbage-grade financial products, and eventually burdened the public with their imprudence through an unprecedented bailout. Nakamoto believed that in a society of strangers, trust can be a liability. It had to be done away with.

This thought is not foreign to political philosophy. In writing *The Confidence Man*, Melville had been inspired by Thomas Hobbes.[8] In Hobbes's state of nature, in which everyone is a stranger, there is always the possibility of distrust. In fact, Hobbes insisted that we should always be on our guard, for you can never be sure whether someone is trustworthy. Because there might be con men among us, we have to fear anyone we meet. Hobbes's *Leviathan* is a solution to the state of nature that resolves the problem of trust. By handing over our rights to the sovereign, we get security in return, which allows us to confide in strangers. We can now be confident that whoever transgresses the social contract will inevitably be sanctioned, which thus makes cooperation with strangers much easier. Yet, Hobbes dismissed the positive function that trust and trusting others can have in society. Trust plays an important role in cementing interhuman relationships. Empirical evidence suggests that we are social animals[9] and our sense of trusting each other is embedded in our existence from the moment we are born, enabling us to undertake beneficial forms of cooperation. Researchers of evolution and child psychology have found that without the initial emergence of mutual trust and toleration—for example, in voluntarily tempering competition for food and demonstrating willingness to share—the choice for humans to collaborate would not be possible.[10] As Bowles and Gintis observed in *A Cooperative Species*, while humans may act like rational, self-interested, and competitive *homines economici* under market conditions with complete contracts, social preferences including fairness and concern for others' well-being has an important function for societal survival in the many other settings where contracts are not complete.[11]

Trust, Confidence, and Systems

Sociologists have extensively discussed trust, particularly in response to the well-known reflections on trust by systems theorist Niklas Luhmann.[12] Luhmann considered the necessity of distinguishing between *familiarity*, *trust*, and *confidence*. He believed that the trust we exhibit to a loved one is quite different from the trust we exhibit when we interact with a stranger. In the former case, we actually trust the person, intentionally putting ourselves in a situation of vulnerability—and thus blaming us, and the loved one, if that person ends up betraying our trust. In the latter case, we do not trust the stranger as such but rather rely on a series of societal systems (e.g., the legal system and associated enforcement authorities, a set of community norms and peer pressure) that contribute to increasing the confidence in the good outcome of the interaction. This is what Luhman calls system trust, or more colloquially, confidence. If the stranger acts against our interest, we will not feel a sense of betrayal because we never trusted the stranger; rather, we will recalibrate our confidence in the system or systems that brought us to interact with the stranger. In other words, while confidence plays a similar function as trust in that it brings us to interact with others, it is different because confidence does not involve a sense of risk or vulnerability but rather a sense of predictability due to individual expectations toward the functioning of a system.

Perhaps the most important takeaway from the academic discussion on trust and confidence is that these are rich and ambiguous notions, with no single established definition. Rather than trying to come up with a reductive account of these terms, let us try here to delineate the differences between the two terms.

From Luhmann's systems theory perspective, humans, groups, and societies are systems interacting with their respective environments. These interactions are characterized by a sense of familiarity—everything that humans recognize as part of their lifeworld—and unfamiliarity, the strange. The unfamiliar entails a certain degree of uncertainty, requiring mechanisms to cope with this uncertainty. As Luhmann describes, medieval Christian societies accomplished this by means of religion, whose function was to bring the unfamiliar within the theological worldview that was more familiar to believers. Even accidents would be regarded as fate or as the will of God. This changed with the secular notion of *risk*, which turned uncertainty from a matter of fate into something that would potentially lie within the control of human agency. What scholars generally agree upon is that both trust and confidence are means to cope with uncertainty in terms of risk. However, the former involves accepting the risk and engaging in a situation of vulnerability toward the trustee, whereas the latter involves creating systems to reduce uncertainty and therefore decrease the risk associated with a particular situation.

Hence, while the two phenomena share a common basis and are, to some extent, interdependent, they remain significantly distinct from one another. The most extreme form of trust exists between people with strong ties, especially family members and friends. People who benefit from those ties can take conscious risks by establishing trust dependencies and acting altruistically, making themselves vulnerable to betrayal.

Moving away from this extreme form of interpersonal trust, we encounter trust between citizens of a political community, conceptualized by Pettit[13] as "civility," a general sense of benevolence and civic mindedness cultivated by peer pressure and reputation. This type of trust is not grounded in emotion but is a rational and voluntary process, similar to what Hardin[14] called the rational evaluation of "encapsulated interest." The idea here is that trust exists as one expects that fellow citizens have a desire for establishing a trust relationship because it is in their own rational interests to do so. Still, these forms of civic trust don't operate as well in a large-scale setting, as evidenced by Melville's story of the confidence man. In an open society of strangers, civility or encapsulated interest often stands on shaky grounds, and one might easily fall prey to a swindler.

We move on to what Luhmann calls "confidence." Confidence rests on shared expectations, which are not simply the result of a leap of faith—as in the case of trust—but are supported by a particular understanding of the world that is regarded as sufficiently predictable as to remove any sense of uncertainty and therefore risk. Confidence can emerge both from general or embodied knowledge (e.g., our confidence in cryptography is based on our understanding of mathematics) or repeated experiences (e.g., our confidence that the sun will rise every morning is grounded on the fact that we have experienced it all our life). Confidence can also be intentionally constructed by creating sociotechnical systems specifically designed to constrain or regulate parts of the environment in order to make them controllable—like through the use of law enforcement or the physical walls of a prison. Often, these two mechanisms overlap. Consider, for instance, the monetary system. Confidence is key to this system as people will only accept money if they expect it to constitute an effective means of payment and that its value will be relatively stable to acquire goods and services over time. At the same time, the monetary system is a sociotechnical system with central banks controlling the issuance of currency and setting bank interest rates, among other things, and regulators ensuring that loans are sufficiently collateralized and clients' funds are properly held in custody. As such, the monetary system, along with its key players and regulatory authorities, allows strangers to interact with one another—even without any prior trust relationships—because it builds up confidence based on a set of shared expectations of a (seemingly) predictable system.

Yet, as the 2008 global financial crisis has shown, confidence in the monetary system is still based on underlying trust relations. Some of these relations are akin to a problematic form of encapsulated interests (e.g., reputation of bankers depending on extreme risk-taking behavior); others are linked to specific trust relations between bankers and politicians. This seemingly predictable system can suddenly breach our expectations or even *betray* us when we realize that we have made ourselves vulnerable to the whims of corruptible or unreliable financial institutions or other trusted authorities.

This underlying layer of trust has become fairly visible, for instance, when payments toward Wikileaks were blocked by the major American payment providers in 2011,[15] revealing that we inadvertently trusted these intermediary authorities, which have the authority to decide whether and how our money can be spent. This is precisely when Nakamoto's invention truly proved its worth, for it allowed people to bypass the ban of these providers and continue to support Wikileaks by sending payments in Bitcoin. The confidence in the operations of the Bitcoin network is thus, at least apparently, much more significant than the confidence we put in the traditional financial system.

The Confidence Machine

What the Wikileaks episode suggests is that Bitcoin is a technology that produces confidence without the need for underlying trust relations. While it has often been stated that blockchain is a "trustless" technology that purports to eliminate the "need" for trust,[16] it has not been clear from the outset what would *replace* the trust that is removed. Similarly, the claim that this technology replaces trust in a *known* other with trust in an *unknown* other[17] does not provide sufficient insight of the nature of trust in systems. From the discussion above, it becomes clear that the blockchain is a "confidence machine."[18] What this means is that a blockchain establishes robust shared expectations between participants interacting through it by means of a combination of technologies that create and maintain a high degree of predictability regarding the blockchain's operations. Because of this, participants can adopt an "unquestioning attitude" toward the technology, not having to take any conscious risk regarding its basic operations. That is, once a transaction is made, one can feel confident that the transaction will execute as expected, without the risk of any interference from a third party.

While the technical features of blockchain technology have been explored in chapter 2, we need to consider how these produce the confidence implied in the notion of a confidence machine. The question thus becomes how blockchain technology maintains a high degree of predictability in its operations, without trusted intermediaries. Answering this question revolves around considering three aspects of the workings of blockchain technologies:

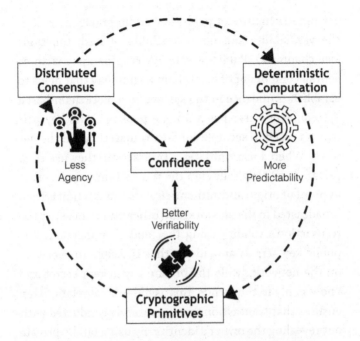

Figure 5 The confidence machine. *Source:* Primavera De Filippi, Morshed Mannan, and Wessel Reijers, "Blockchain as a Confidence Machine: The Problem of Trust and Challenges of Governance," *Technology in Society* 62 (August 2020): 101284, https://doi.org/10.1016/j.techsoc.2020.101284.

(1) cryptographic primitives, (2) deterministic computing, and (3) distributed consensus (figure 5).

First, blockchain technology relies on cryptographic primitives (well-established, low-level cryptographic algorithms commonly used in cryptographic protocols) to create predictability. This predictability comes from the asymmetric nature of public-key cryptography as well as the verifiability and nonreversibility of hash functions (see chapter 2). Public-private key cryptography is an essential component of blockchain technology that helps to establish confidence in the system. In a blockchain-based system, every user has a unique public-private key pair, which is used to securely conduct transactions on the network. When a user initiates a transaction, they use their private key to digitally sign the transaction, which serves as proof of origin and authenticity. The transaction is then broadcasted to the network, and other users can verify the transaction's validity using the sender's public key. The public key acts as an address that is visible to everyone on the network, while the private key is kept secret and known only to the owner. This asymmetrical relationship ensures that transactions can be securely conducted without revealing the owner's identity. By using public-private key cryptography, blockchain-based systems ensure that only the rightful owner of a digital asset can initiate transactions and prove their ownership. This feature adds a layer of security and confidence to the system as users can be assured that their assets are protected from unauthorized access or fraudulent activity.

Hash functions are another fundamental component of the confidence machine as they generate a high level of predictability concerning the immutability of data recorded on a blockchain. Hash functions are mathematical algorithms that take an input of any length and produce a fixed-size output known as a hash, or a "digital fingerprint." In a blockchain-based system, each block contains a hash of all the transactions included in the block as well as a hash of the previous block in the chain. This creates an unbreakable link between blocks and ensures the immutability of transactions recorded into a blockchain, as any change in a single block would result in a different hash, invalidating the entire chain's integrity.

Second, deterministic computation suggests there is a one-to-one relation between the inputs and outputs of any blockchain transaction. This stems from the fact that computer code deployed on a blockchain executes in a formal, nonambiguous, and deterministic manner. As such, it brings a degree of predictability that is absent from natural language: a message transmitted to blockchain code leaves no room for interpretation and will always result in the exact same outcome. This is a critical feature of blockchain technology as it ensures that all nodes on the network can independently verify the validity of transactions and maintain the blockchain's integrity.

Third, blockchain technology relies on distributed consensus to extend the determinacy from a single computer to that of a network of nodes, ensuring that every node will produce the same order of transactions. This generates a high level of predictability that transactions are unambiguous not only in terms of their content but also in terms of their chronological order. Distributed consensus algorithms constitute the basis for a decentralized peer-to-peer validation of transactions, leveraging economic incentives to ensure that all peers in the network cooperate toward maintaining and operating the network, with no incentives to free ride. To be sure, this only works under the assumption that all miners are rational, utility-maximizing economic agents who only act to maximize their profits and are therefore highly predictable in their behaviors.

Together, these aspects ensure a high level of predictability and therefore confidence in the system. As Nick Szabo argued, blockchains seek to substitute "rust in the secret and arbitrarily mutable activities of a private computation" with "verifiable confidence in the behavior of a generally immutable public computation."[19] As discussed in chapter 2, Szabo, in developing the concept of the smart contract, invoked the analogy of the vending machine. A vending machine is a highly deterministic mechanical system that is fully predictable: throwing in a coin in the machine will give access to the selected product. The technology envelopes a "mechanical contract" rather than a legal one. Hence, rather than relying on the legal system and police force to guarantee the legal contract's execution, the technological infrastructure of the vending machine guarantees the execution of the mechanical contract. There is thus no longer any need for trust, nor (ex post) enforcement, as the contract is automatically executed by technological means, at least in theory.

Bringing Trust Back In

Just as any other sociotechnical system, vending machines are liable to the tricks of confidence men. There is outright vandalism, which vending machines can be protected against, but there are also much more sophisticated ways to cheat on them. The point that vending machines are still vulnerable to confidence tricks is brought home by the example of Tommy Glen Carmichael,[20] a famous swindler with a curious addiction. Carmichael was in the habit of finding ways to "cheat" on the vending machine's close relative: the slot machine. He would dissect slot machines at home, learning about their inner workings, to find a way to circumvent them. This is how he developed the "Monkey Paw," a flexible tool made, among other things, of guitar strings that one could slide into a slot machine's payment channel. This would trigger the microswitch controlling the payout channel, resulting in all the cash to be released. Despite being caught and put in prison, Carmichael kept his addiction and was in constant competition with slot machine makers. When the industry produced a new machine that used a sensor to keep track of the number of coins that were paid out, Carmichael invented the "light wand," a light that would blind the sensor, thereby disabling it. He would sell his inventions to other con men on the dark market, wreaking havoc on the gambling industry and causing damages amounting to hundreds of millions.

Carmichael's story brings home the message that even though slot machines, like smart contracts, appear to offer fully predictable executions of programmed actions, they can be compromised. And while only a physical tool is needed to compromise the slot machine, there are multiple ways to compromise a blockchain network, which reveal the interdependency between trust and confidence. This can be illustrated by the case of the Steem blockchain,[21] an online social media platform, similar to Reddit or Medium but decentralized. Steem's innovation was a new way to curate content, giving users the possibility to use Steem tokens to upvote and downvote content. The Steem blockchain is governed through distributed consensus, where a set of community members—called "witnesses"—are selected based on their reputation, which they can gain from community votes.[22] The top twenty witnesses are the elected block producers, who are practically in control of the blockchain network's maintenance and operation. At the moment of the launch, however, some of Steem founders locked up a large amount of their tokens, which became infamously known as the "ninjamined" stake.[23]

Enter Justin Sun, a flamboyant and savvy Chinese blockchain entrepreneur, founder, and CEO of the Tron blockchain network. As Sun decided to purchase Steem, he became entitled to the ninjamined tokens, which gave him a significant influence in the governance of the Steem blockchain. As a response, the Steem community voted to implement a soft fork to prevent Sun from accessing and voting with these premined tokens, as a protection mechanism to avoid a hostile takeover. Yet, Sun had a trick up his sleeve. Using his personal influence at some of the major crypto exchanges, he leveraged the Steem tokens held in custody by those crypto exchanges to elect his own trusted witnesses, thereby effectively seizing control over the Steem blockchain.

This is a fascinating episode of a blockchain community trying to prevent one influential individual from taking over a blockchain network, with the "empire striking back."[24] It suggests that trust had not disappeared altogether but had merely been distributed among a network of actors. The role of the exchanges, backing up Sun's claim, demonstrates that even in a decentralized blockchain network, there can be centralized points of failure, enabling individuals to take control over the network. First, some of the initial developers of the Steem blockchain created a trust-based liability by creating the ninjamined stake. More generally, developers and open-source contributors to a blockchain network can have significant influence, not only at the inception phase but also in its course of evolution. Indeed, the production and maintenance of the codebase on open-source platforms like GitHub is typically organized in a considerably centralized and hierarchical manner. While open-source development might seem like a purely technical affair at the outset, it often involves making political choices that steer the operations of a blockchain network.

Second, token holders can exert significant influence on a blockchain network, as illustrated by Sun's large amount of tokens holding, which gave him the means to influence the blockchain governance and elect new witnesses. Finally, external parties like policymakers and regulators can impact the trust relations in the nexus of actors orbiting around a blockchain-based network. For instance, regulators could crack down on the behavior of individual actors like Sun,[25] affecting the extent to which they are trusted by other actors.

It could well be argued that the Steem blockchain was vulnerable because it was an imperfect version of the confidence machine. Its weakness was the design of its consensus mechanism. Leveraging a delegated system instead of Bitcoin's PoW system, it relied on trust relations from the outset. Yet, as we will further explore in chapter 5, even the Ethereum blockchain (which at the time used a PoW consensus mechanism) has encountered a significant breach of confidence, in the aftermath of an incident known as The DAO attack. Also, in more robust ecosystems like Ethereum, trust relations between the different typologies of actors mentioned above impact the functioning of the confidence machine.

Accordingly, while it is clearly the case that blockchain technologies reduce the need for trust and increase confidence in the system, it is wrong to describe them as trustless systems since trust can never be eliminated. Rather, trust is distributed among a network of actors, making it difficult for any single actor to unilaterally breach the rules of the system. Exceptional events like the Steem takeover have brought the underlying trust relations to the surface. Instead of denying the existence of these trust relations, blockchain proponents would therefore do better to account for the role that trust plays in these systems—which can be seen as both a strength and a liability. Trust is a liability when trust relations undermine the integrity of a blockchain network, for instance, in the way that Sun leveraged his connections at major exchanges. Yet, it can also help saving and strengthening the integrity of a network, for instance, by providing the basis for a community to react against an attack (as will be discussed in chapter 5).

The moral of the story is that trust in the governance of a blockchain-based system is necessary for it to qualify as a proper confidence machine. To manage this trust, blockchain communities must leverage both on- and off-chain governance strategies and solutions. On-chain solutions to improve trust in governance may involve implementing new types of consensus mechanisms or more robust voting systems, which off-chain solutions may involve procedural and substantive modes of community governance. For instance, procedural safeguards could be put in place to determine the course of action of key actors like core developers and major token holders deciding on a recommended protocol update.

*　*　*

By way of a discussion of trust and confidence in sociology and political theory, chapter 4 questioned the alleged trustless nature of blockchain technology. It showed that blockchain technology should rather be regarded as a confidence machine that displaces trust without, however, eliminating it. The chapter elaborated how the cultural values and political beliefs of actors involved in the governance of a blockchain can impact newfound trust relations. Trust, it turns out, still plays an important role in—and emphasizes the importance of—blockchain governance. In the next chapters, we will explore these and other forms of blockchain governance, which are aimed at managing the underlying trust relations for the sake of making the confidence machine operate more effectively.

STATES OF EXCEPTION

The exception is more interesting than the rule. The rule proves nothing; the exception proves everything.

—Carl Schmitt, *Political Theology*[1]

Waiting for Barbarians

The magistrate rules over a sleepy frontier settlement at the edge of a vast empire. For as long as he can remember, the settlement had been peaceful and prosperous. One day, however, a man by the name of Colonel Joll arrives, who represents the empire's powerful intelligence service. The magistrate recounts their first meeting: "We do not discuss the reason for his being here. He is here under the emergency powers, that is enough."[2] In his novel *Waiting for the Barbarians*, the Nobel Laureate John M. Coetzee thematizes a long-standing debate in legal and political philosophy about the relation between political power and the state of emergency. He recounts how the "emergency" has to do with an imminent threat: the possibility of a barbarian insurrection. This threat justifies the application of powers that would otherwise be beyond the purview of the law, including horrendous torture. The state of emergency necessitates *suspending* the law to deal with a situation that the normal legal order is supposedly incapable of addressing. Coetzee was inspired by a poem of the same title by the Greek poet Cavafy, which concludes with a twist: at the end of the day, the barbarians never arrive. "Now what's going to happen to us without barbarians?" Cavafy writes, "Those people were a kind of solution."[3]

The poem's twist reveals something important: the empire does not merely respond to an emergency to protect itself from outside danger; rather, the palpable risk of an emergency constitutes its power to continue to exist. As the magistrate muses, "one thought alone preoccupies the submerged mind of empire: how not to end, how not to die, how to prolong its era."[4] In the first half of the twentieth century, the controversial[5] German legal theorist Carl Schmitt developed his concept of politics by building on a similar intuition, namely that the origin of political power lies in the existential distinction between friend and enemy. The enemy, the "barbarian," is not only a threat but also necessary for political power to sustain itself. The

The state of emergency necessitates *suspending* the law to deal with a situation that the normal legal order is supposedly incapable of addressing.

reason is that whoever has the ultimate decision-making power in a political system, the sovereign is he "who decides on the exception."[6] The enemy represents the latent possibility of the *exception*, an unlikely event or act that threatens the sovereign. Deciding on that possibility is, according to Schmitt, what politics is all about.

But what is the exception? There is no straightforward answer to this question. Perhaps, with Taleb,[7] we might say that it is like a "black swan": a high-impact, extremely low-probability event that comes as a surprise. One such event would be the 9/11 terror attacks on the World Trade Center. Being a unique historical moment that shook the foundations of the Western world, it was also the pretext for the Bush administration to proclaim a state of emergency—suspending parts of the law to reduce citizens' rights and extend the state's coercive and surveillance capabilities. As with the discussion of the concept of confidence in chapter 4, the discussion concerning the exception is closely related to our understanding of the predictability of the world. For Schmitt's claim to work, we must accept the possibility of something truly surprising, as a predictable event or action can, at least in theory, be assimilated by the law.

Hans Kelsen, an influential Austrian legal philosopher, considered the law as a system of legal norms that cover things that might happen in the world. It operates in an "if-then" fashion. If you steal, then you will be sanctioned.

This system knows a hierarchy: lower-level laws about particular events are subsumed under higher-level, more general laws. At the highest level, Kelsen hypothesized the existence of a "basic norm,"[8] a norm that exists outside of the legal system but also stabilizes it. The actual law that would reify this basic norm is the constitution. All laws would derive their validity from the basic norm, and the test of validity would be one of logical deduction: if a lower-level law contradicts a higher-level law, it is invalid. This theoretical system, known as "legal positivism," is what Kelsen favored and Schmitt attacked. Schmitt believed that it tried to get rid of politics, creating the illusion that the application of the law is devoid of any genuine decision-making. Kelsen, he believed, proposed a self-regulating system, a legal machine of sorts. The sovereign "had been pushed aside" because now the "machine runs itself."[9]

In the summer of 2016, a less scholarly version of this debate raged on the Internet about the first DAO built on the Ethereum blockchain, known as The DAO. The DAO was intended to be an unstoppable organization, a machine that runs itself. It was not ruled by corporate statutes and codes but rather was governed by self-executing smart contracts and blockchain code.[10] Yet, like a true digital Titanic, The DAO sank on its maiden voyage. The unstoppable code was exploited by an attacker, who amassed a large portion of the cryptocurrency stored in the smart contract. While some powerful actors in the Ethereum eco-system effectively called for a state of emergency, others disputed the need for any intervention as the vulnerability was a part of the codebase. And, after all, the "code is law." The central question in these debates was if the siphon-ing off of USD 150 million equivalent of cryptocurrency amounted to theft and was thus an exceptional event that the existing codebase could not address without external intervention. In challenging the norm that code is law, had the blockchain barbarians arrived?

The Code Runs Itself

The DAO was a first-of-its-kind experiment in on-chain governance, which refers to rules and decision-making procedures that are encoded into the infrastructure of blockchain-based systems. An example of such a rule is the cap on Bitcoin quantity, which ensures that no more than 21 million Bitcoins will ever be created. Similarly, an on-chain decision-making procedure can be illustrated by Bitcoin's PoW consensus mechanism, which is used to validate transactions on the blockchain. The DAO was de-signed to operate as a distributed crowdfunding platform that would replace the arbitrary coercive power vested in traditional platform operators like Kickstarter with what we characterized in chapter 3 as the *rule of code*. Any of the globally distributed token holders of The DAO would be able to propose new projects that people could invest in, and the decisions made through this decentralized governance system would be executed "autonomously" through smart contracts.

To envision how this might work, take the example of an apartment rented through a DAO that simulates the Airbnb platform. When renting a place on Airbnb, you need to use a centralized payment system such as PayPal to transfer funds to the host. Then, you must receive a physical key or an apartment code, which can occasionally become problematic. For instance, if the key isn't handed over upon arrival, you would have to find alternate accommodation and possibly enter into an arbitration procedure to recoup any costs and damages. When operated through a DAO, you would instead enter into a smart contract linked to a physical "smart lock" attached to the property. Once you enter into an agreement through The DAO to rent the place, everything would happen automatically: an amount would be deposited from your account on a smart contract, allowing you to unlock the smart lock when you arrive. At the end of your stay, the deposit would automatically be returned to you minus the rent, and you would no longer be able to unlock the door.

In fact, this type of solution was the one proposed by the developer team of Slock.it, the company that proposed and built The DAO. Beyond automating access to a property, The DAO could do much more. Using a combination of on- and off-chain governance tools, token holders could even directly make decisions that are usually taken by a board of directors, like how to distribute dividends from profits made through the platform. In short, it could potentially encompass all governance functions of a platform like Airbnb by means of self-executing rules of code.

What type of "legal order" does a DAO implement, and what would establish the validity of a "law" in such an order? Striking similarities can be established between the legal positivism established by Kelsen and the principles underlying a DAO's design. According to Kelsen, the validity of a law cannot be derived from its content. The description of "John opens the cash machine in the neighborhood shop, takes out $200, and runs away" does not by itself qualify as an act of *theft*. For this, one needs a norm that forbids stealing. Conveniently, software code is both descriptive and performative, being able to combine a statement with a normative, deontic operation (e.g., allowing, forbidding, restricting). Similar to Kelsen's test of validity, the validity of a transaction on a DAO is not derived from the transaction's content. Instead, it is derived from the norm encoded in, for instance, a smart contract that determines whether a transaction can or cannot be made.

But if the validity of a rule is derived from a norm, where does the validity of that norm itself come from?

Kelsen argues that "the reason for the validity of a norm can only be the validity of another norm."[11] This is why he had to make the hypothesis of the existence of a "basic norm," one that needs no further validation. It is real-world constitutions that articulate and represent the basic norm "by presupposing the basic norm . . . one ought to behave as the constitution prescribes."[12] For a DAO, the most basic rules are those laid down in the blockchain protocol (in the case of The DAO, this would be Ethereum). The blockchain protocol thereby expresses a higher-level basic norm that all participants tacitly presuppose.

If blockchain-based systems like The DAO implement a legal regime similar to Kelsen's characterization of a positive legal order, would they also be vulnerable to Schmitt's critique? Schmitt contended that by its very nature, an exception cannot be legally determined in advance. Hence, decisions must first establish whether there indeed is an exception and, second, determine how to manage it. According to Schmitt, the issue is that legal positivism attempts to dissolve these political decisions in an impersonal system, like the system of parliamentarism that subjects all decisions to procedures that have to be followed (e.g., majority requirements in voting). These procedures could allow decision-making to dissolve into endless discussion, affecting the effectiveness of governance. This is fine in normal situations, which allow for lengthy negotiations between particular interests (e.g., child safety advocates versus gun rights advocates in the US). Yet, when an emergency arises—such as an insurrection—we don't have the luxury of channeling decision-making through such a system because an urgent decision becomes *necessary*. And such a decision, Schmitt contends, is taken by a personal agency that arises out of the impersonal system, a latent sovereign power that cannot be cast aside.

Schmitt's claim has an empirical basis. Most states have constitutional provisions that allow for the executive to suspend the normal legal order by declaring a state of emergency. Consider, for instance, the emergency powers enacted in France after the 2015 terrorist attacks, which, according to some, led to a "permanent state of emergency," suspending the basic rights of certain groups.[13] One historical example stands out, which was also the direct object of the dispute between Kelsen and Schmitt: the fall of the Weimar Republic in 1933. The Weimar Republic, established after World War One, stood out in having a progressive positivist constitution that sought to vest sovereign power in the parliament, the Reichstag. Yet, it allowed for the executive office of the president to use emergency powers in line with the infamous "Article 48." This article outlined that the president could overrule regional governments, if needed by using the armed forces, and suspend basic rights. This could happen in case a regional government would not fulfill its duties or if public security were at stake.

As Dyzenhaus explained, right-wing conservative forces in Germany coalesced to turn the country from a democracy into an authoritarian state.[14] In 1932, Article 48 was invoked on multiple occasions to dissolve the Reichstag, which necessitated an election that turned Adolf Hitler's *Nationalsozialistische Deutsche Arbeiterpartei* into the largest party, and to incapacitate the regional social-democrat government of Prussia. Once Hitler had gained the office of chancellor, he used the burning down of the Reichstag building, allegedly caused by communist terrorists, as a pretext to suspend constitutional rights. Subsequently, he eliminated the communist faction of the Reichstag and passed the Enabling Act, which vested all sovereign power in the office of the chancellor, making him the de facto dictator of Germany. While the fall of the Weimar Republic was a product of political conspiracy and violence, a crucial role was played by the constitution itself. While it contained many safeguards (e.g., measures invoked under Article 48 could be revoked by the Reichstag), the constitution was vulnerable to the state of exception. Primarily, it is the sovereign that has the agency to decide on whether there is a state of exception to begin with—which is disputed in the case of the Reichstag fire in 1933. As the magistrate explains about the role of the empire's emissary Colonel Joll in staving off the barbarian threat, he is there to "find out the truth. That is all he does."[15] This truth does not pertain to what *is* the case but to what *ought* to be the case.

The DAO Attack

The DAO attack has been a pivotal event in the Ethereum community because it brought out a tension that goes right to the core of the underlying blockchain technology, namely whether its presumed immutability can or should prevail over human agency. Immutability, it turned out, is not an inherent feature of a blockchain but rather a norm underpinning its management and operations. This norm is similar to what Dyzenhaus claimed is the underlying concept of Kelsen's legal positivism, namely "that no individual should be subject to the will of any other individual or group of individuals,"[16] in the sense that the law should also not be unilaterally changed subject to the capricious whims of any single human agent—including the sovereign herself.

What precisely occurred during The DAO attack? Let us turn to a chronological depiction of events. On April 30, 2016, The DAO was deployed on the Ethereum blockchain and a four-week crowdfunding period followed in which funds were raised through an ICO. Anyone could send Ether to The DAO and receive The DAO's native tokens in exchange. During this time, the community also discussed proposals for ways that DAO funds might be spent.

Well before The DAO went live, concerns were raised about potential vulnerabilities in the code base and its governance. A proposal was published on May 26 by the

Slock.it team itself for updating The DAO's security and appointing a security expert. Despite these concerns, at the end of the crowdfunding period on May 28, The DAO went live. It had amassed a staggering capital contribution, worth approximately USD 150 million in cryptocurrency. On June 5, a new technical vulnerability was discovered in The DAO's code that would enable a potential attacker to repeatedly call a vulnerable withdrawal function and siphon assets before the smart contract's balance could be updated. In light of this discovery, the Slock.it team started to work on an update of The DAO that would solve this vulnerability as well as other security issues. On June 12, the company released a statement stating that "no funds were at risk." Yet, on June 17, an anonymous user exploited this vulnerability to drain The DAO's funds, siphoning 3.6 million ETH (approximately USD 60 million at the time) from The DAO's smart contract to another DAO controlled by the attacker.

Once actors in the Ethereum ecosystem became aware of this attack—following an alarming message posted on Reddit—they started to coalesce behind a closed Slack channel to discuss counterstrategies. The immediate step was to get the main cryptocurrency exchanges to agree to halt trading of The DAO native tokens. Due to a safety feature of The DAO's smart contract, the funds in the new DAO were "frozen" for approximately twenty-seven days,[17] giving the Ethereum community an opportunity to identify a suitable solution. On June 18, a message was posted,[18] allegedly originating from the attacker, invoking the *code-is-law* mantra and claiming that the siphoned funds were to be regarded as a "reward" for making the community aware of this vulnerability.

In the weeks following the attack, different solutions were brought forward by the Ethereum community. Some of these were "soft forks" that would not violate the protocol of the Ethereum blockchain but would rather instruct clients to ignore any transaction originating from the attacker's DAO. Yet, these solutions were found to have serious security risks, because they would enable malicious users to spam the Ethereum blockchain. The other option was a "hard fork," which would effectively violate the rules of the Ethereum protocol, making the forked chain backward-incompatible with the original chain. The hard fork consisted of forcing a transfer of funds from the attacker's DAO to a newly created smart contract, whose function was only to enable the original token holders to withdraw their funds. This latter option was considered by many as the safest way to remediate the "theft" and was actively supported by Vitalik Buterin and other core members of the Ethereum Foundation.

On July 20, the hard fork of the Ethereum network occurred. Most mining nodes adopted the new client, indicating support for the newly created version of Ethereum that had remediated the theft. Some, however, kept mining blocks for the original Ethereum blockchain, which had now been renamed as "Ethereum classic." Heated discussion ensued about the fork's legitimacy. Some argued that it was an unjustified violation of the network protocol because the attack had executed exactly as prescribed in the code, with no consequences for the Ethereum blockchain. Others, however, argued that The DAO attack had been a reality check, urging the community to rethink its governance in light of myriad potential smart contract vulnerabilities.

The debate surrounding The DAO attack, in a rudimentary way, resonates with similar debates occurring almost a century earlier between legal philosophers. First, there is the question of the state of exception. Was The DAO attack sufficiently disruptive for Ethereum to justify the declaration of a state of exception? The answer to this question should not be merely descriptive but also normative, including consideration of whether the Ethereum network had operated as it *ought* to. As Schmitt foresaw, this question cannot be answered by the system itself as it requires the exercise of agency by a focal point of sovereignty. Influential agents came together to agree on a strategy to address such an exception, before strategizing on tackling the exception. The majority advocating for a hard fork proactively proposed a way to handle the exception. Given its lack of backward compatibility, the hard fork is comparable to a constitutional change that establishes a new constitution. Yet, a radical departure from the classical debate on the state of exception is the fact that the fork led to the establishment of two alternative versions of the Ethereum blockchain. This would be similar to supporters of the original Weimar constitution having maintained their own republic despite Hitler's separate regime of terror. In the physical world, however, this is simply not an option.

Taming the Specter of Private Interests

In the case of a "normal" hard fork, a standardized procedure is followed that relies on a formalized off-chain proposal process with checks and balances. Even if imperfect, this workflow is in line with legal positivism's ideal that no individual or group of individuals can arbitrarily force their decision upon the network. The hard fork in the aftermath of The DAO attack, however, was unplanned and could not—due to the urgency of the exception—follow normal procedures. While nodes still could not be coerced into joining one chain over another, they were confronted with a narrow range of choices to choose from and high economic stakes resting on their choice. It thus revealed the existence of a latent network sovereign, a focal point of agency distributed among a few influential individuals and groups, who effectively limited the choices available. Ultimately, what The DAO attack has shown is that blockchain systems are also vulnerable to what Schmitt described as the "coalescence of private interests."

Speaking of liberal democracies, Schmitt argued that the "machine that runs itself" (i.e., the positivist legal order) is concerned more with the validity of laws, including those that establish a community's shared values, than with the substance of those laws. For instance, such an order lays down formal requirements for a proposal to be issued, the voting mechanism to approve proposals, and thresholds for a proposal to pass. In a liberal, pluralist society, any value is as worthy of being considered as any other; a shared conception of the common good is absent. One can hold the opinion to want to abolish public education, spend all public funds on combating climate change, or even abolish democracy as long as this opinion is directed through the proper procedural channels and the laws enacting these views are valid. Thus, Schmitt argued that even though the system does lay down a basis for formal legality, it fails to provide a ground for substantive legitimacy—as an additional justification of its own rules. The legal order can distinguish between valid and invalid rules and decision-making procedures but not between "right" and "wrong" that derive from a substantive understanding of the common good.

For this reason, the only way that the legal order in a liberal democracy can produce a common good is through negotiations and discussions between private parties and the state, which is subsequently enacted through legal procedures. Private interests have to coalesce to gain power in this negotiation, in configurations ranging from foundations to lobby groups. A blockchain network faces the same fundamental challenge. Whenever questions arise that go beyond mere technicalities and involve some notion of the common good, private interests may come together, creating a focal point of sovereignty that in extreme situations might even undo the integrity of the blockchain itself. Hence, despite its claim to immutability, blockchain technology cannot fundamentally ignore the role that governance, particularly off-chain governance, plays in its operations. To avoid potential abuses resulting from the coalescence of invisible powers, blockchain communities would do well to recognize the role of off-chain governance as a complementary and powerful force and ideally put in place specific mechanisms for constraining governance.

One possible change would be a new procedural mechanism. This means establishing a formalized governance process for handling exceptions, as exists in traditional political orders and constitutions. The implications of establishing such a procedural solution can be illustrated with reference to the event known as the "Parity bug."

The Parity bug was a vulnerability in the library smart contract code of Parity multisig wallets (i.e., wallets that require multiple signatures to authorize transactions). In

November 2017, an anonymous attacker exploited this vulnerability to gain control over the library smart contract with the sole purpose of destroying it by calling the *self-destruct* function. All multisig wallets that depended on this library thus became inoperative, resulting in the freezing of more than USD 150 million worth of Ether at the time. The incident significantly impacted Ethereum governance as it highlighted the importance of code audits and security measures in blockchain technology. It also led to a debate within the Ethereum community about the best way to handle such incidents and whether or not it would make sense to again intervene by means of a hard fork to bring the smart contract library back to life, thereby enabling the frozen funds to be returned to their rightful owners. Ultimately, in contrast to the decision taken in the aftermath of The DAO attack, the Ethereum community decided not to implement a hard fork, thus preventing anyone from retrieving the frozen funds.

The reasons for this decision are multifaceted. First, the actual amount of Ether involved in the Parity incident was much lower than in The DAO attack (500,000 ETH versus 3.6 million ETH). Second, while a decision on The DAO attack had to be taken within a short time frame, the community had a longer time frame to consider their approach to the Parity bug. Third, and perhaps most importantly, the Parity bug didn't affect Ethereum overall but was a more isolated security failure regarding a particular smart contract. But who is to decide on the severity of a network crisis? Who has the power to decide whether the execution of a smart contract, albeit perfectly compliant with the rule of code, should be reverted in the name of rule of law concepts like theft or protection of private property?

A more robust, formalized, and transparent governance system appears to be desirable as it could specify an appropriate mechanism for deciding and resolving exceptions. A range of governance approaches could be adopted, from preserving the informal status quo to implementing forms of delegation. In the latter, a community agrees on the rules and constraints that establish an "emergency regime." This assigns a narrow set of powers to a predefined group of delegates to frame approaches to resolving an exception, which network actors will then consider and implement.[19]

However, formalizing such a procedure comes with problems if not approached carefully. For instance, if the Ethereum community were to establish a particular regime for fund recovery, assigning broad powers to a predefined group of delegates over whether or not to reverse a transaction, this would mean officially giving up on the immutability guarantees of the Ethereum blockchain. While these powers could be formally limited in terms of time (e.g., emergency decision-making powers for a defined period, extended by majority vote of community) and scope (e.g., excluding particular types of decisions), this would only tame but not prevent the emergence of a new latent sovereign power in a system that was precisely designed to be devoid of any sovereign. It would also involve abandoning commitments to decentralization since such a mechanism would, by design, involve coercing other network actors.

It is for this reason that several blockchain communities have begun adopting off-chain governance mechanisms that are substantive in nature, most notably drafting "constitutions" and "codes of ethics" to articulate shared values that they agree to be bound by even in the absence of coercion. A commitment to features like decentralization and ethical approaches like "inclusiveness" not only help cultivate "civic values" but also involve substantive processes that require moving beyond preserving the positivist legal order encoded in a blockchain protocol or DAO.

* * *

Departing from a discussion of blockchain as a code-based legal order that "runs itself," this chapter turned to legal theory to expose the challenges raised by states of exception in blockchain-based systems. It outlined the scholarship on sovereignty and the state of exception, focusing on the works of Kelsen and Schmitt. It continued with an exposition of The DAO attack, elaborating on the events and actors involved in this state of exception. Blockchain technology—despite its promises—does not eliminate all risks of centralization through coalescence of private interests, meaning that the specter of the exception remains. The next chapters will delve deeper into the kind of legal order generated by blockchain technology, questioning the extent to which it is alegal and how it may produce both legal and legitimate forms of governance.

ALEGALITY

Every command slaps liberty in the face.
—Mikhail Bakunin, *Oeuvres*[1]

Pax Bitcoinica

What would it be like to live in a libertarian utopia? Imagine you are a digital nomad, living in what Balaji Srinivasan calls the network state of Bitcoinica. You wake up in an apartment belonging to Bitcoinica and decide to fly to another property owned by this network state in the city of Berlin. At the airport, you identify yourself to the authorities with your Bitcoinica passport, which uses zero-knowledge proofs to verify your Bitcoinica citizenship without requiring you to reveal other personal details. You then travel to the Bitcoinica makers' hub in the neighborhood of Kreuzberg, where you make payments to a Bitcoinica smart contract to reserve desk space and buy coffee. At your desk, you use your private key to enter the Bitcoinica metaverse, where you can work and unwind with Bitcoinica citizens from all over the world.

In the summer of 2022, the former chief technology officer of Coinbase, Balaji Srinivasan, captured this futuristic idea in a manifesto. Srinivasan argues that we find ourselves in a pivotal moment, in which humankind should shed the nation state in favor of the network state.[2] There are several prerequisites for the formation of his network state. A network state needs a social network, a moral proposition that defines its purpose, a recognized founder, a virtual capital, its own cryptocurrency, and a real-time census of the population and accounting of its assets. Additionally, it needs encryption and a blockchain network for the state's administrative infrastructure. It also requires a national consciousness among citizens, the ability to act collectively, a high degree of civility within the network, and the consensual conferral of a limited, withdrawable set of privileges assigned to the governors in exchange for admission to the state. The last, but potentially most significant feature, falls within the domain of international law: the diplomatic recognition of the network state by other existing states.

Srinivasan's audacious call for an online community to bootstrap an entire state could be dismissed as a form of speculative fiction. Yet, the new political imaginary it invokes is only possible due to the substrate provided by blockchain networks. The intuition is that if the creation and circulation of Bitcoin can wrest control over monetary and financial policy, then "self-sovereignty" in other domains could also be attainable—including the eventual creation of entirely new states. That he considers Bitcoin to be a type of global sovereign is clear from his coining of the term *Pax Bitcoinica* to describe how Bitcoin, through its very existence, becomes a government of governments, as it "sits above every state and constrains it from printing infinite quantities of money, from lawlessly seizing the funds of its citizens, and from waging forever war. In doing so, it limits that which will never limit itself."[3] Bitcoin, in other words, is above the law and can never be brought within its fold: it is alegal.

The Notion of Alegality

In 2014, Gavin Wood delivered a presentation on the concept of alegality. After having asked the audience what they understood by the term, he explained that it was "something which just doesn't care . . . cannot care . . . as to whether its actions might be interpreted as legal or might be interpreted as illegal."[4] As public blockchain networks do not have a centralized operator or a CEO, they cannot be shut down through take-down requests or forms of litigation. It is too costly to sanction hundreds, if not thousands, of geographically dispersed and pseudonymous users. For Wood, each of these systems are therefore like an unregulatable "force of nature": actions taken through blockchain systems would subsist outside of any legal order and thereby provoke a change in what is deemed to be illegal. On the one hand, the use of these distributed systems would make it *easier* to enforce certain existing laws (e.g., AML regulations, if financial transactions were executed on-chain). On the other hand, it would make it *harder* to prevent mutually beneficial agreements that are freely agreed upon. As a consequence, Wood predicted that blockchain would force us to rethink our existing legal system.

In the years since Wood's talk, the term "alegal" has quietly been adopted by crypto enthusiasts and interpreted in different ways. It has been used to explain the ambiguous or silent position of states to the legality of Bitcoin as well as to contend that alegality can be leveraged to achieve political objectives. Most significantly, the concept of alegality inspired the creation of The DAO a few years down the line.[5]

As Wood readily concedes, he was not the first to coin the term alegality or develop it conceptually. Legal scholars have developed the concept of alegality to argue how an act can be irreducible to the legal/illegal binary that is maintained by the state apparatus. Hamzić describes this as the capacity to "exist and act in the interstices, or perhaps beyond or outside, the dominant modes of . . . legal production."[6] For Lindahl, the scholar who has written most extensively on this concept, alegality denotes a "strangeness,"[7] which contributes to alegal acts being unintelligible to the law. While Lindahl primarily had human actions and behavior in mind when elaborating on the concept of alegality, Wood raised the question of whether systems like open blockchain architectures can also be alegal.

To better appreciate this line of thinking, it is necessary to understand what Lindahl means by legal order. He defines legal orders as "institutionalised and authoritatively mediated collective action."[8] This means that collective action is regulated by certain authorities on behalf of citizens through the framing and enforcement of rules. Most citizens are therefore expected to agree to a common set of rules as well as the authorities responsible for regulating collective action, irrespective of the identity of any particular individuals who hold official positions within these authorities.

According to Lindahl, legal orders possess temporal, spatial, material, and subjective boundaries that establish the distinction between legality and illegality.[9] While ordinary legal and illegal acts can readily be circumscribed within this binary, alegal acts test these boundaries and, on occasion, trigger changes of these boundaries. In other words, legal and illegal acts reinforce existing legal boundaries, while alegal acts open the possibility of innumerable alternative legalities.

Laws are temporally bounded in the sense that they specify *when* acts can be done and when they cannot. This is most clearly seen in the general legal principle that laws should only apply prospectively, not retrospectively. Relatedly, despite laws striving to be "future proof," in reality they cannot account for all possible future acts and developments. Thus, an alegal act that would breach the temporal boundary of the law would be one that initiates something new and unprecedented in that legal order—such as the creation of Bitcoin or the founding and recognition of Bitcoinica as a network state.

The spatial boundaries of the law demarcate the physical territories *where* acts can and cannot be carried out. These territories may be contiguous to the territorial boundaries of a nation state or may be archipelagos distributed across the globe, subject to the authority of a multinational corporation.[10] Even cyberspace is physically embedded, with e-commerce platforms relying on physical places like warehouses, the seller's point of shipment, and the buyer's home. Alegal acts that transgress spatial boundaries are those that question where it is legal or illegal for an act to occur. Asylum seekers—some of whom will be granted refugee status and others who will be deported—tangibly test these spatial boundaries with every crossing, as they raise political questions about whether this act of crossing should be legal or illegal.

Material boundaries of the law circumscribe *what* acts can be carried out in a certain time and place and are usually articulated as sets of rights and obligations.[11] The various peoples' tribunals charging leaders (e.g., Putin) and states (e.g., Myanmar) with international crimes do not have formal, state-backed jurisdiction to try such crimes, but they give visibility to rights violations that are ignored by national and international justice systems due to procedural reasons or geopolitical considerations. The deliberations and verdicts of these tribunals may be alegal, but they shape public opinion and make it possible to envision the operation of a different judicial system, one with alternative conceptions of justice.[12]

Finally, the law's subjective boundaries set *whose* acts can be permitted or sanctioned. A citizen is the most obvious example of someone who can be subject to a legal order, but even the nature of their status may differ based on their residence or criminal record. If a citizen is resident outside of their home country or possesses a criminal record, they may be excluded from certain rights of citizenship, like standing in a national election for an official post. These subjective boundaries can be challenged by an alegal act that questions existing prohibitions or restrictions on who can act in a given context, with the intention of changing the terms of these prohibitions or restrictions. The storied legacy of brave slaves who participated in the slavery abolition movement—at great risk to their own lives—is a powerful example of people taking actions to have their personality and subjecthood recognized by an existing legal order.

Alegal acts not only test boundaries but also affirm the role of boundaries as *limits* of a legal order, limits between the "collective self and other-than-self."[13] In the case of a limit, legislative action or, in certain limited ways, courts can redraw the boundaries of a legal order to domesticate the alegal act. But in some situations, legal reform or judicial interpretation are not enough. In these instances, the boundaries of legal orders instead appear to be *fault lines*, which means that trying to domesticate the alegal act would threaten the core identity of the legal order.[14] We can think of coexisting and parallel civil and personal law regimes as an example of this, where changes to the status quo would require choosing between two norm-based systems that are deemed to be equally legitimate. As with many countries, India has laws derived from its various religious communities governing issues such as marriage and property inheritance, but there have long been debates about replacing this complex patchwork of personal laws with a uniform civil code that would provide a common set of rules on these matters. Considering such legislation—not to mention actually passing it into law—appears as a fault line as it puts into question the identity of the legal order itself.

Boundary transgression occurs through three broad categories of alegal acts. First, there are acts that are alegal in Wood's sense in that they are practically not possible to include within a legal order, for example, the biological process of thinking. Second, there are alegal acts that are intelligible to a legal order and can be addressed through legal reform to adjust the law's boundaries. For instance, copyright law reform can tackle digital piracy. Third, there are alegal acts that create fault lines because they are unintelligible to an existing legal order; attempting to incorporating them would require a wholesale overhaul of both the law's boundaries and norms. Blockchain systems provide an illuminating example of the latter two categories, which will be discussed more fully in the next section.

Destructive Golems

To what extent do blockchain networks facilitate alegal acts that create fault lines? Initially, the answer seems to be that blockchain networks are not alegal in this sense if we consider the actions of some powerful actors in blockchain networks. Intermediaries, like centralized cryptocurrency exchanges, have been subject to significant legal and regulatory action. This is partly because these intermediaries, operated by corporations and executives, can readily be brought within a state's jurisdiction (e.g., through injunctions, arrests), and partly because they engage in activities that are already governed by the law (e.g., money transmitter regulations). Their actions can therefore more readily be classified as being legal or illegal, as can be seen in the spate of litigation against various crypto exchanges over the years, from Mt. Gox to FTX.

Similarly, ICOs and other broad-based fundraising schemes have long been a feature of blockchain networks. These ICOs have typically been organized by a centralized entity and involve activities that are analogous to fundraising schemes of the past. Thus, when allegations of securities fraud or other criminal acts arise, it is trivial to frame charges and pursue legal action against them. The application of the long-standing *Howey* test in the United States—derived from a case concerning whether the sale of interests in an orange grove amounted to an investment contract—to contemporary token offerings, to ascertain if they are investment contracts and thus unregistered securities, indicates that regulators and courts can pierce through the technical and financial complexities of a case to grasp the economic realities of a transaction. In other words, merely using new packaging for an investment does not qualify it as being an alegal act, as legal interpretation can be used to reinforce the law's boundaries.

Even more elaborate crypto businesses, like Celsius Network, which pays interest to users who deposit cryptocurrencies with them, fail to be alegal in this third, stricter sense as they have centralized operators. These operators can be charged with crimes that can be committed in a wide and open-ended variety of ways. For instance, in 2022, Celsius Network's operator was charged with grossly mismanaging funds and fraud for artificially setting the price of its native token and not managing risk properly. Because of this, users have not been able to withdraw their deposited cryptocurrencies but, as of November 2023, a reorganization plan has been confirmed by the US Southern District of New York Bankruptcy Court pursuant to which account holders will (according to Celsius) eventually receive about USD 2 billion. Some of the allegations made about businesses like Celsius Network and FTX include activities already regulated by well-established bodies of law. While illegal acts can, in some instances, be alegal if they strive to change the boundaries of a legal order, this intention is not present in many of these cases. In short, many of the activities popularly associated with the running of a blockchain-based system, from initiating an ICO to operating a crypto exchange, do not create fault lines.

Yet, when focusing on the core design of blockchain networks, the claim to alegality becomes more credible. Take, for instance, the transparency and tamper-resistant qualities of blockchain protocols. Because of these features, it is exponentially difficult for content to be removed from a widely used public permissionless blockchain regardless of whether that content is harmful (e.g., child pornography), questionable (e.g., pirated content), or considered publicly beneficial (e.g., on-chain financial transactions of sanctioned Russian oligarchs). More importantly, blockchain transparency and tamper-resistance can transform how issues like financial transparency are regulated altogether. Imagine, for instance, legal authorities using blockchain analytics to trace the transfer of crypto assets that they suspect of being used for criminal purposes and thereby enforcing a new regime of financial transparency, such as the one introduced in the EU through the Transfer of Funds Regulation in 2023. Whether desirable or not, this resonates with what Wood meant by the alegal nature of blockchain systems prompting the reimagination of how illegal activities are regulated. Blockchain technology thereby prompts us to test the material boundaries of the law and can prompt a reconfiguration of how rights and obligations are distributed in a legal order.

Blockchain also challenges the law's subjective boundaries. Consider the novel "property regime" of crypto assets. In traditional property regimes, ownership titles are defined and granted by the law, with the state acting to enforce those laws should a false claim be made about ownership. Physical possession, while important, is not the be-all and end-all of determining who has legal ownership. In contrast, the novel property regime in blockchain systems is captured by the aphorism "not your keys, not your coins." It is possession of one's private key associated with a crypto wallet that makes one *technically* the owner of the cryptocurrency in that wallet, as it allows one to exercise the rights typically associated with full ownership, such as access, transfer, and use. As the FTX debacle revealed, ownership of a crypto asset does not necessarily lead to the enjoyment of ownership rights. FTX held many users' crypto assets in FTX wallets, and when the exchange went under, many users lost access to their crypto holdings. It became unclear for many whether they would be able to regain control over their crypto assets. After all, there is no guarantee that a court will enforce legal ownership. For instance, a 2020 case in California involved a claim by a user alleging that financial gains from the forking of their crypto assets were not passed on to them by their crypto custodian. This claim was not upheld by the court as the custodian held the tokens, and the contractual agreement between the user and the custodian gave the latter discretion in passing on financial gains from forked assets.[15] While legal and technical ownership remain in tension, judgments such as these seek to encompass transgressive legal acts within the law's boundaries.

Moreover, blockchain challenges the spatial boundaries of the law. As The DAO (see chapter 5) was not controlled by a centralized operator and was not registered in any state, it existed simultaneously everywhere and nowhere. In this respect, blockchain-based systems differ from traditional entities that depend on registration in, or at least recognition by, a territorial jurisdiction. Even in this age of ubiquitous multinational corporations, this connection between an entity and a territory determines an entity's capacity to interact with the physical world. The recognition of the separate legal personality of unregistered DAOs without requiring registration in a state would amount to a redrawing of the law's spatial boundaries and require significant political and administrative changes.

The DAO Model Law developed by the Coalition of Automated Legal Applications (COALA) calls for this approach, asking jurisdictions to eschew local registration requirements and instead recognize alternative functionally and regulatorily equivalent means for achieving the policy objectives of registration. Whether such a deterritorial approach is adopted remains to be seen. The state of Utah's DAO Act, based on The DAO Model Law, does waive registration requirements and recognizes unregistered DAOs meeting certain conditions as equivalent to domestic LLCs. However, it maintains a physical link to the jurisdiction by requiring that a registered agent be physically present in the state of Utah.

Finally, blockchain challenges the law's temporal boundaries. Consider the decision to pursue a hard fork of the underlying Ethereum protocol in the wake of the attack on The DAO. While the retroactive unwinding of undesirable past transactions at a set point in time addressed the concerns of those who considered The DAO attack to be a form of theft, others believed this act infringed the code-is-law approach. This act was alegal as it raised fundamental questions about the sequence of how and when acts are appropriately done. It just so happens that the coordinated action to hard fork led to an outcome that made victims of theft whole. In several subsequent hacks of blockchain protocols, such coordination did not occur, and the law could not command a hard fork to occur either.

These examples show how the design of blockchain networks enables them to resist the force of legal orders in certain ways and even prompt the redrawing of legal boundaries. Despite its limitations, Wood's claim regarding the alegality of blockchain technology raised an interesting question: can blockchain systems be alegal by design? To some extent, this seems to be the case. While most scholars of alegality have limited the concept to purely political actions, it seems that systems like blockchain do have politics, as Winner famously argued.[16] By mediating human action, a blockchain can allow actors to transgress the boundaries of the law, thereby leveraging design to enable alegality.[17] Yet, despite this capacity, and contrary to Wood's claim, it is far from the case that

Can blockchain systems be alegal by design? To some extent, this seems to be the case.

blockchain networks do not or cannot care about traditional legal orders. Indeed, even blockchain-based systems specifically designed to enable alegal acts are invariably entangled with state legal orders.

One example of this is Tornado Cash, a blockchain-based software system used to enhance financial privacy. Users can send cryptocurrency to Tornado Cash smart contracts from one address and then withdraw it to another, thereby severing the link between the two addresses, obfuscating the holder's identity, and retaining control of the cryptocurrency. This service can be used for both legitimate and illegitimate purposes, ranging from anonymous charitable donations to the funding of hackers. What makes Tornado Cash distinct is that it is a collection of smart contracts on the Ethereum blockchain without a centralized operator that can stop or intervene in its operations. This was a deliberate choice by the founding team of developers, as they wished to preserve the immutability of the smart contracts and enable Tornado Cash to be trustless and autonomous—a true confidence machine—thereby upholding the "precepts that code is law."[18]

The technological affordances of Tornado Cash allow it to perform alegal acts that transgress all four boundaries of the law. Since its deployment, it has challenged the temporal boundary of the law by a novel, more censorship-resistant system of preserving financial privacy. Simultaneously, this system challenges the law's material boundaries by strengthening the right to financial privacy at a time when it is threatened. By concealing the origins of financial transactions, Tornado Cash enables individuals to perform otherwise unfeasible transactions, such as making outward remittances in jurisdictions with strict foreign payments restrictions, thereby challenging the law's authority on who may or may not take certain financial actions. Finally, as with unregistered DAOs, since Tornado Cash is a collection of smart contracts that exist everywhere and nowhere, it transgresses the spatial boundaries of the law by challenging any state's ability to claim jurisdiction over it.

At least this is what appeared to be the case. On August 8, 2022, and November 8, 2022, the US Treasury's Office of Foreign Assets Control (OFAC) sanctioned Tornado Cash for facilitating a North Korean hacker group to launder proceeds from their activities. As a result of these sanctions, it became unlawful for any US citizen, resident, or company to conduct transactions with the smart contract addresses linked to this blockchain-based service, which held more than USD 400 million worth of Ether at the time. While OFAC claimed that this sanction targets the Tornado Cash "entity," comprised of its founders, developers, and DAO, at the time it appeared to target a list of smart contract addresses. This means that no one, including the development team, has control over its operations, and therefore there is no way to modify or shut it down. Can code be sanctioned? Following the sanction order, centralized GitHub repositories were removed, the Tornado Cash DAO went dark, and a developer was arrested in the Netherlands. However, the Tornado Cash smart contract addresses continue to autonomously process transactions that are sent to it. As a result, these sanctions were heavily criticized, especially within the blockchain community, as they effectively apply to a technological artifact rather than to a legal entity.[19]

On the one hand, the example of Tornado Cash shows how legal boundaries can become fault lines. What some claim as being a sanction that targets a group of persons, others perceive as being a sanction of autonomous code. Thus, the sanction could potentially fall foul of existing liberal approaches to regulating software code as speech, which is protected by the constitutional right to freedom of speech in the United States.[20] To address this fault line, some have called for fundamental and drastic change. For Farrell and Schneier, the Tornado Cash imbroglio necessitates a revisiting of the long-established doctrine of considering code as speech. Tornado Cash, they argue, is a "destructive Golem" (referring to the mythical artificial creature in Jewish folklore created from inanimate matter). This Golem can exist and mix transactions for as long as the Ethereum blockchain exists, leaving a long trail of broken laws and regulations in its wake.[21] In their view, only some code is speech, and speech that collapses speech and action in the manner that a DAO does should not be protected as speech.

On the other hand, the sanction notices demonstrate the limits of alegality. It is true that the law cannot directly alter code on the blockchain. Yet, it is clear that sanctions can indirectly regulate the persons who interact with sanctioned addresses. In the case of Tornado Cash, these targets of regulation include the block producers who process network transactions as well as cryptocurrency exchanges. Soon after the sanction notices were announced, more than 50 percent of Ethereum block producers were, by default, censoring transactions that originated from Tornado Cash irrespective of whether they were legally subject to the sanction.

In contrast to Srinivasan's vision of blockchain-based systems acting as a government of governments beyond the reach of any legal order, technologies that are alegal by design like Tornado Cash show that such systems are entangled with state legal orders in complex ways. While legal orders can imprison developers, frighten validators and cryptocurrency exchanges, and stifle the development of privacy-enhancing technologies, the Tornado Cash smart contracts themselves continue to function. While some hope that sanctions and regulation will disable this autonomous Golem, it is unclear how these will be enforced, and it is uncertain that all stakeholders will otherwise voluntarily comply. If these systems continue to progressively become more decentralized and diverse, it will become harder to imprison the Golem. As a case in point, after months of most block producers censoring transactions emanating from Tornado Cash, by April 2023, the majority of them could use non-US software—clients and relayers—to process these transactions despite the OFAC sanctions remaining in place.

* * *

Drawing on legal theories concerning alegality, chapter 6 explored how the design of blockchain technologies enables them to resist the force of legal orders, transgress legal boundaries, and even redraw them. For techno-optimists, the alegal nature of blockchain technologies is worth preserving as it allows certain freedoms and rights to be extended, such as the right to financial privacy. Blockchain alegality seemingly offers a way to be free from legal commands that—as the anarchist Bakunin put it—"slap liberty in the face."[22] A more pessimistic view is that without sweeping regulation and reform, autonomous systems will devolve into destructive Golems that cause widespread social harm. Given the limits of what the law can unilaterally achieve in the context of blockchain networks—and the crises blockchain networks routinely experience—the following chapter shows how the need to cultivate perceptions of legitimacy can motivate actions that are in the community and public interest.

LEGITIMACY

The most important scarce resource is legitimacy.

—Vitalik Buterin, "The Most Important Scarce Resource Is Legitimacy"[1]

Polycrisis

In 2022, as Russia launched its war on Ukraine and the global economy experienced the aftershocks of the COVID-19 pandemic, the world of crypto also experienced a "polycrisis." After some major stablecoins collapsed, the NFT market crashed and the market cap of most public blockchains dropped dramatically. The biggest shock would come with the downfall of the crypto wunderkind Sam Bankman-Fried and his FTX empire. Enter the crypto winter.

In these precarious times, the legitimacy of current governance practices come into question, testing confidence in existing institutional arrangements. The crypto winter has also raised questions about legitimate governance in the blockchain space. The debate on this topic was already initiated in 2021, at the height of the crypto boom, by Ethereum founder Vitalik Buterin. On his personal blog, Buterin argued that blockchain proponents had overlooked a very important factor in governance: the pattern of higher-order acceptance that he called legitimacy.[2]

What Buterin argued is that as technically sophisticated as a blockchain system might be, it still requires a certain degree of acceptance to function at all. Buterin claimed that legitimacy can derive from various sources depending on context—including brute force, continuity, fairness, process, performance, and participation. Yet, he noted that the legitimacy of blockchain-based systems was particularly dependent on higher-order acceptance by all network participants of the outcomes of the system, which he argued was mainly built around the expectation that others will also accept these outcomes as being legitimate.

In seeking to define legitimacy, Buterin unwittingly entered into conversation with the many scholars who have theorized legitimacy, the German sociologist Max Weber being the most notable one.

Legitimacy and Legality

Weber considered legitimacy to be the *acceptance of authority* and the *requirement to obey commands*. He developed a conception of legitimacy that was concerned more with how a political system designs rules and delegates power in line with these rules than with what these rules substantively say. The legitimacy of a political system arose from people being accustomed to its practices and mores (i.e., tradition), their trust in the exceptional qualities of a leader (i.e., charisma), or their confidence in a rational set of rules and norms being followed (i.e., legality). In this sense, legitimacy derived from legality depends on conformity with procedural rules and "technological choices, not ideological ones."[3] Any value or principle that has been embodied in law can be regarded as legitimate.

For other scholars, like Dyzenhaus, legitimacy and legality are intertwined concepts, but the existence of the latter does not necessarily entail the existence of the former.[4] From this perspective, the existence of legitimacy requires more than legality as it implies that people also *accept* the rules established through law. Habermas and Heller, for instance, argue that the legitimacy of the law is derived from the fact that it is democratically produced.[5] In traditional democracies, the acceptance of rules and authorities often stems from free and fair elections. When citizens participate in elections and choose their representatives, they are more likely to accept the decisions and laws passed by those representatives as they have contributed to the selection process and can hold their officials accountable. However, democratic accountability alone is insufficient. Acceptance also requires a well-functioning judicial system that upholds the rule of law. When people believe that laws are applied consistently and fairly, without favoring those with high status or power, they are more likely to accept and respect those laws. Transparency also plays an important role in building acceptance. When government actions and decision-making processes are open and accessible to the public, it fosters trust and accountability in the governance process, thus increasing the likelihood that its outcomes will be accepted.

As a consequence of this distinction, an action or a governance system can be perceived as legitimate—at least by a segment of the population—even when it is explicitly unlawful. Consider the case of exchanging copyrighted content over the Internet, which some may view as legitimate despite its illegality. The same holds true in the context of blockchain-based systems; many activities there are regarded as legitimate even if they violate the protocol's rules. For instance, a hard fork can be considered legitimate because it allows for the possibility of innovation and evolution within a particular blockchain ecosystem. Essentially, forking is a way for a blockchain community to decide (i.e., to vote) on how the blockchain

When government actions and decision-making processes are open and accessible to the public, it fosters trust and accountability in the governance process, thus increasing the likelihood that its outcomes will be accepted.

should be upgraded and what direction it should take. Hence, even if the resulting network does not adhere to the original protocol, it can still be perceived as legitimate because it represents the community's will. Of course, as The DAO attack (chapter 5) has shown, not everyone might agree that a fork is legitimate, particularly those who equate legitimacy with legality and consider that such an action is an unlawful demonstration of political power. Contentious forks might thus result in the emergence of two separate networks (e.g., Ethereum versus Ethereum Classic) that compete with each other to acquire the highest level of legitimacy and therefore adoption.

Another interesting example that illustrates the potential disparities between legality and legitimacy in the blockchain space is the case of MEV, which refers to the total value that can be extracted from a set of transactions in a blockchain network. MEV arises due to the presence of various economic incentives and opportunities that can be exploited by miners and validators in the network. It can become a significant challenge in public, permissionless blockchain networks like Ethereum, where multiple actors with varying degrees of power and autonomy interact. These include miners, validators, searchers, and users—each with their own goals and incentives. If these actors compete with each other to extract MEV, this can lead to suboptimal outcomes for the network as a whole.

For instance, a block producer may prioritize certain transactions over others based on their potential for MEV. While this is consistent with the rules of the underlying blockchain protocol, it can create a sense of unfairness for those who submitted transactions that were deprioritized. Additionally, the pursuit of MEV can incentivize block producers to engage in activities that may undermine the network's overall security, such as reordering transactions to maximize their gains.

The legality of MEV practices is generally clear—at least within the legal orders of blockchain systems—as they operate within their established rules and protocols. However, its legitimacy is a subject of ongoing debate and controversy.[6] Many within the Ethereum community question whether the pursuit of MEV aligns with the broader principles of fairness, decentralization, and security that the technology seeks to uphold. This debate underscores the nuanced nature of legitimacy in the blockchain space, where practices that may be legally permissible can still face scrutiny and ethical considerations from a legitimacy standpoint.

To address these challenges, various solutions have been proposed among the Ethereum ecosystem, including implementing MEV-focused protocols such as Flashbots and adopting gas auction systems that allow users to bid for priority in transaction processing.[7] However, these solutions are still in development, and the governance of MEV remains a significant challenge in blockchain networks.

Different Shades of Legitimacy

In the context of blockchain systems, distinguishing between endogenous and exogenous legitimacy is essential for understanding how these networks are adopted. Endogenous legitimacy refers to legitimacy that arises from within the blockchain ecosystem itself. It is based on the network's internal mechanisms, consensus protocols, and adherence to predefined rules and governance structures. When participants within the blockchain community collectively agree on the network's governing rules and processes and have confidence in its security and reliability, endogenous legitimacy is established.

Conversely, exogenous legitimacy pertains to legitimacy that arises from interactions with actors outside the blockchain ecosystem. This form of legitimacy is often influenced by external factors, such as the need for regulatory compliance and legal recognition by traditional institutions. Exogenous legitimacy can be vital for bridging the gap between blockchain technology and broader socioeconomic and legal systems. When blockchain projects work within established legal frameworks, obtain regulatory approvals, and collaborate with recognized institutions, they can enhance their exogenous legitimacy, which can in turn boost confidence and adoption among a wider audience. At the same time, if the blockchain community were to compromise on the ecosystem's fundamental rules and social norms (e.g., with regard to privacy or decentralization) to comply with external rules and regulations, the gain in exogenous legitimacy could result in an erosion of endogenous legitimacy.

Balancing both endogenous and exogenous legitimacy is therefore crucial for blockchain systems to thrive and gain acceptance in a rapidly evolving and interconnected world. In turn, acceptance and adoption is crucial as blockchain networks depend on the existence of network effects for their value and security. In this section, we will analyze the various ways in which blockchain systems might enhance their endogenous and exogenous legitimacy.

First, as proposed by Mittiga, it may be useful to distinguish between two separate forms of legitimacy: *foundational* and *contingent* legitimacy. Foundational legitimacy pertains to a government's ability to ensure the safety and security of its citizens, whereas contingent legitimacy subsists in situations in which governments "exercise power in acceptable ways."[8] While the existence of contingent legitimacy depends on the situation in question, this might include a combination of procedural and substantive factors,[9] such as "the presence of democratic rights and processes, consent, guarantees of equal representation, provision of core public benefits, protection of basic individual rights and freedoms, social justice, and observance of fairness principles."[10]

Applying these concepts in the context of blockchain technology can shed light on the multifaceted nature of legitimacy in these polycentric systems. Foundational legitimacy in a blockchain system relates to the system's ability to guarantee a secure and effective technological infrastructure. This comprises a blockchain's technical aspects, such as its cryptographic security, consensus mechanisms, and resistance to attacks. A blockchain with strong foundational legitimacy is one where participants have full confidence in the safety and integrity of the network— that is, one that can be successfully assimilated to a "confidence machine."[11] Conversely, contingent legitimacy in a blockchain system arises from how the governance and decision-making processes are conducted within the network. Similar to traditional governance settings, this form of legitimacy depends on both procedural and substantive factors. These include the type of decision-making mechanisms (e.g., democratic, plutocratic, meritocratic), the concentration of decision-making power, the representation of different stakeholders in the network's governance, the protection of individuals' rights to privacy and freedom of expression, and so on.

In essence, while foundational legitimacy is concerned with the technical decentralization, robustness, and security of the blockchain system, contingent legitimacy addresses political decentralization and how power and authority are wielded within the network. A blockchain network with both foundational and contingent legitimacy is more likely to be accepted, and therefore adopted by the masses, because in such networks the underlying governance of the network is addressed to ensure that the technological guarantees of the network are not compromised.[12] Thus, enhancing the foundational legitimacy and contingent legitimacy of a blockchain system is likely to have a positive effect on both endogenous and exogenous legitimacy.

Yet, even if there is evidence of endogenous legitimacy, at the exogenous level, more normative conceptions of legitimacy might require evidence that blockchain systems guarantee the protection of basic human rights.[13] For instance, Schneider has argued that some of the various regulatory levers described in chapter 3 could be used to promote human rights. Market competition between various blockchain systems could be based, among other factors, on their commitment to human rights and environmental stewardship. Social norms among developers may evolve, leading to greater peer pressure to consider such factors when working on new updates to a blockchain system. As regulation in this space proliferates, legislators might include basic rights and environmental protection requirements for network actors (e.g., to permit miners to operate).[14]

To an extent, norms are evolving and market pressures are emerging that encourage tackling environmental harm and creating sustainable energy markets. A large proportion of PoW miners have shifted to using renewable energies, and some are arguably helping balance loads on electricity grids and reducing energy waste.[15] Blockchain-based regenerative finance projects are gaining attention as an alternative to DeFi and offering opportunities to invest in clean energy, carbon offsets, and social enterprises.[16] In some places, like New York State, a stricter regulatory approach has been adopted by placing a two-year moratorium on PoW mining that uses nonrenewable energy.[17] When a public authority considers various regulatory options—which are partly targeted at achieving strong exogenous legitimacy—it is important for the authority to evaluate whether they may possibly jeopardize the endogenous legitimacy of these systems by weakening its foundational properties and technological guarantees.

Another way of conceptualizing different types of legitimacy was provided by Schmidt, who distinguished between *input legitimacy*, *throughput legitimacy*, and *output legitimacy*. Input legitimacy is based on a governance system's responsiveness to citizens' concerns (i.e., governance by the people), and output legitimacy is determined by the effectiveness of a governance system's policy outcomes (i.e., governance for the people). Throughput legitimacy depends on the quality of governance, as determined by the responsiveness of a governance system to "citizens' input demands while ensuring the best possible policy outputs."[18] Accordingly, even if a governance system enjoys strong foundational legitimacy and contingent legitimacy, it may nonetheless lose its legitimacy if its outcomes consistently fail to meet the expectations of those it serves. Black has shown that perceived output legitimacy might be based on *pragmatic* grounds (i.e., the outcomes directly or indirectly pursue one's personal interests), *moral* reasons (i.e., the outcomes are perceived as being morally appropriate), or simply on the basis that they are *cognitively necessary* or *inevitable*. For instance, when a cyclone strikes an area, its citizens may accept drastic measures to save people, such as ordering the evacuation of homes.[19] Legitimacy is thus clearly a relative concept: what is legitimate in one context may not be legitimate in another.

Regarding output legitimacy in blockchain systems, participants may find pragmatic reasons to consider the system legitimate as long as it consistently delivers on its promised functionality. Block producers, for instance, receive economic rewards for their participation in maintaining the network, aligning with their financial self-interest. In exceptional situations, such as The DAO attack, participants may opt to endorse one fork over the other based on moral reasons (e.g., the belief that theft should not go unpunished). Additionally, they may cognitively accept a fork as an inevitable intervention that is necessary to preserve the network's security and sustainability. A blockchain system may be perceived as having input legitimacy to the extent it can adapt and respond to the changing needs and concerns of the various stakeholders involved. The system may also have throughput legitimacy when it not only incorporates its participants' voices and preferences but in doing so also effectively adapts to the changing technological and economic landscape.

Blockchain systems do not always enjoy throughput legitimacy. The Bitcoin scaling debate has shown the difficulty for a blockchain network to implement a significant protocol change, thereby failing to respond to the demands for a greater throughput of transactions.[20] The challenge in this case was that given the polycentric nature of public, permissionless blockchain systems, different stakeholders with their own vested interests might have very different expectations as to how a blockchain should operate or evolve. Any change in the network also incurs the risk of generating unexpected and unforeseeable consequences that might ultimately decrease the network's output legitimacy. The same is true with regard to endogenous and exogenous legitimacy, where attending to the expectations of external policymakers and regulators to gain more input legitimacy (e.g., by supporting know your customer [KYC], AML, or counterterrorist financing [CTF] regulations) might ultimately impair the blockchain system's throughput and output legitimacy from the perspective of internal stakeholders.

Blockchain Constitutions

The use of the constitutionalism lens to explore the legitimacy of blockchain-based systems may appear surprising at first, but it is less so when we consider how conformity with higher-order rules is one of the essential sources of these systems' legitimacy. As discussed above, beliefs about how others will act in a given situation are shaped by the technical and game theoretical rules embedded in a blockchain-based system. Protocol rules, such as consensus mechanisms, provide the basis on which the validity of new blocks can be tested. However, these on-chain rules may sometimes lack instructions about rulemaking on certain issues and principles that articulate a community's shared values and norms—a gap that can make these systems less adaptable to change and emergencies. Without expressly articulating a system's shared values and core principles, predictions about how others will act becomes more fragile and harder to anticipate. On-chain governance can become unreflective of developments off-chain, and the existence of Schelling points cannot be taken for granted. For several blockchain projects, the solution was articulating a constitution in an off-chain written document, stipulating a series of secondary rules on how primary (on-chain) rules are to be made, amended, or removed, along with a set of guiding principles. A constitution can serve several purposes, including the design of governance institutions,[21] that is, specifying the legal basis and extent of the powers assigned to different actors, and providing the narrow conditions under which these arrangements can be changed.

While states are the ones typically associated with constitutions, nonstate actors are also progressively adopting these documents. The ICANN (Internet Corporation for Assigned Names and Numbers) is a prominent example in this regard. To assign domain names, ICANN brings together a constellation of state and nonstate actors within a governance system that has its own dispute resolution system as well as its own set of secondary rules (i.e., rules on how to make rules). As a consequence, some scholars argue that ICANN has created its own constitutional order.[22] This claim has been buttressed by recent work in the field of digital constitutionalism, which argues that large, multinational tech firms like Meta are undergoing a process of constitutionalization[23] and in doing so ought to incorporate the values of contemporary liberal democracies into their constitutional orders, including adherence to the rule of law and upholding human dignity.[24] It is from these conceptual developments that the notion of "blockchain constitutionalism" has emerged.

Some scholars argue that blockchain networks already have constitutional rule sets and constraints enshrined into the protocols.[25] This "formal" constitution, articulated through software code, sets the terms of what *is* and what *isn't* permissible on the network and, as mentioned in chapter 3 (rule of code), guarantees that these rules cannot be unilaterally changed by any network participant. The formal on-chain constitution of Bitcoin also embodies certain core principles, such as a limit on the number of Bitcoin that will ever be emitted.

The on-chain constitution is not set in stone as there is always the opportunity to fork a blockchain protocol, thereby exerting a "competitive pressure" on the previous protocol.[26] Moreover, not all elements of a blockchain constitution exist on-chain: the constitution of many blockchain networks also comprise formalized off-chain procedures like BIPs for Bitcoin and EIPs for Ethereum, as well as a series of informal norms and customs. These off-chain processes are instrumental to critical blockchain governance debates and are likely to inform the community's course of action regarding any proposed changes at the protocol layer.

As with state constitutions—where the formal constitution always faces pressures to represent the "actual relations of forces" in the state (i.e., forces exerted by the interests of capital, the working class)[27]—blockchain-based systems also face pressures to reconcile their "formal" constitution with their "material" one. The on-chain formal constitution may not accurately represent the principles and beliefs of a blockchain community as it lacks the flexibility to reflect these principles in natural language. Furthermore, it may lack a mechanism to understand and enforce these principles. This is where formal off-chain constitutions come in.

A written constitution, in an ideal sense, would bridge the on- and off-chain elements of blockchain governance and enable a tighter and more responsive connection between the formal constitution recorded on-chain and the more tacit material constitution that mostly subsists off-chain. For instance, the Ethereum Naming Service (ENS) protocol (i.e., Ethereum's equivalent of the Internet's Domain Name Service system) is governed by a constitution that provides "binding rules that determine what governance actions are legitimate for the [ENS] DAO to take" as well as the quorum and supermajority voting requirements needed to amend the constitution.[28] Over 84,000 accounts signed the constitution, and as a result, DAO governance proposals are only supported if they align with the ENS DAO Constitution.

As Tan and colleagues show, many of these documents also articulate more general principles and values held by the community (with openness, inclusivity, and decentralization being common themes).[29] In the case of the 1Hive DAO (a community of Web3 builders), the goals and principles that guide the community are complemented with a dispute resolution system that allows the interpretation of whether community values are being upheld, providing a way of addressing ambiguity that is not possible through purely on-chain governance. Recent disputes in 1Hive have invoked specific clauses of the community covenant (i.e., fostering a healthy community economy) to challenge the legal validity (i.e., constitutionality) of resource allocation proposals that would allegedly lead to unhealthy outcomes. This dispute resolution process bears a strong resemblance to the process of judicial review, where ordinary legislation is tested for compliance with the constitution.

As with political governance, there is more than one path toward enhancing a blockchain system's legitimacy. Optimistically, the drafting of such constitutions would enhance the endogenous legitimacy of blockchain systems as they would explicitly articulate shared values. These shared values, and being able to collectively enforce these values, can contribute to strengthening the pattern of higher-order acceptance that is central to Buterin's vision of legitimacy. More ambitiously, this development can shape new normative conceptions of legitimacy that further people's freedom and human rights.

A more pessimistic outlook would be that such constitutions are aspirational at best and dead letters at worst. In lieu of more blockchain constitutions having robust, yet distributed, enforcement mechanisms, value statements could potentially create new sources of community discord (e.g., for not being sufficiently representative) or even legal risk (i.e., for potentially creating new types of liabilities on the participants to the network). This could, perversely, undermine the legitimacy of a blockchain-based system. However, as Alston and colleagues argue, these different approaches to, and debates about, constitutionalization open up competitive dynamics among different governance systems. In competing to offer legitimate governance systems, we anticipate that best practices will emerge on the design of blockchain constitutions.[30]

* * *

Drawing from debates concerning the distinction between legitimacy and legality, and the political conception of legitimacy, chapter 7 critically analyzed the claim that legitimacy is the most important scarce resource of blockchain-based systems. Yet, the role that legitimacy plays in a blockchain system is very different from the role it plays in more traditional, coercive governance structures. By showing that blockchain systems can foster their legitimacy by integrating both on- and off-chain governance processes, this chapter has illustrated the significance of legitimacy in blockchain networks, emphasizing the importance of rules that are not only being legally defined (on- or off-chain) but also genuinely accepted and respected by the community. This was further demonstrated by recent efforts to formalize procedural and substantive constitutional rules in an off-chain document, with a view to improving the overall governance and legitimacy of blockchain systems. As these off-chain constitutional texts proliferate, we argue that it is important for drafters to carefully consider the trade-offs that exist in seeking both endogenous and exogenous legitimacy.

CRYPTOPIA

Man is born free but everywhere is in chains.

—Jean-Jacques Rousseau, *The Social Contract*[1]

(Un)chained

"The car decelerated at the turn. Alina knew how it saw the world: lidar point clouds, IoT sensor oracle feeds, chain IDs—with algorithms predicting where everything was going to be seconds, minutes, days from now." In this snapshot from a short story titled *Unchained*,[2] Hannu Rajaniemi imagines what the future of blockchain might look like. In this future, crypto is not just money or an asset class but a general infrastructure, connecting physical objects like cars with AI agents. The story features a smart car—the Tesla of tomorrow—that functions according to an internal reward system that incentivizes certain uses. It is used by a happy couple who got married using a smart contract that guarantees mutual fidelity. This smart contract is linked with their wedding rings, which are capable of signaling betrayal. One day, Alina's ring reveals her that her partner has cheated on her, and she is now facing divorce. This might seem unremarkable—after all, infidelity is not uncommon. Yet, there's a catch: the smart car's AI system had developed a problematic profit-maximization strategy based on a pattern that cheating couples tended to use the car more. Additionally, it discovered the profitability of selling adultery data to the AI judge that would decide on the termination of the marriage contract. In short, the AI system had generated the incentive to get Alina's partner to cheat and did so by putting him in the car with his perfect match.

The story captures some of the core directions of travel for the future of blockchain technology. To start, blockchain technology is poised to become an infrastructural technology, much like the Internet protocols. This will result from a symbiosis and synthesis with other emerging technologies, most notably with smart devices and AI. Smart devices will allow for blockchains to be integrated into the physical environment, from cars to passports. This also means that physical devices directly become contractual devices. For instance, your future car might be directly governed by a car insurance policy—stored on a smart contract—that keeps track of your driving habits. Integration with AI will then allow smart contracts to not only execute pregiven rules but also condition execution on the machine learning's interpretation of data.

Moreover, this merging of emerging technologies signals the use of blockchain technology beyond the first use case of money. To be sure, this tendency has already been convincingly demonstrated by the use of blockchain for financial products, social media, prediction markets, and so forth. Yet, some of the biggest promises of blockchain—for instance, its use in supply chain management—are, at the moment of writing, still exactly that: mere promises. Once the linking and integration of technologies becomes increasingly successful, the reality depicted by Rajaniemi becomes more likely. This would open the gates toward a society that organizes many of its contractual relations, from commerce to marriage, by means of blockchain technology. It would further accelerate the demise of the ownership society and usher in contractual societies that foster a new sociolegal and political worldview and ideology. As Rajaniemi shows, it may alter our understanding of institutions like marriage and also impact our judgment as humans—given that judgments will increasingly be the function of the execution of a smart contract rather than of our own observations and considerations.

Would this future be a good or a bad one, and what would Cryptopia look like? The answer to these questions is uncertain, but at least three pathways have become discernible. First, blockchain technology might turn out to become the ultimate technology of control, able to put all human relationships not into proverbial, but effective, digital chains. In this tyranny of code, all human activities are liable to rules encoded in one or a few blockchains controlled by plutocratic elites. In this world, there will be a widening gap between the haves and the have nots. Second, the state system might do everything in its power to reel in blockchain technology, diminishing its decentralizing efforts and making it part of the state structure. The clearest example here is the rise of central bank digital currencies, which are now pursued by all major economies. Third, there is the vision of a pluralist world of DAOs, one that echoes some of the utopian ideals of anarchists and cypherpunks like Barlow. In this future, DAOs could both help preserve privacy from surveillance and be responsible for providing various public goods and services, such as health care, education, and environmental sustainability.

TL;DR

As this book has shown, blockchain governance engages core concepts and challenges that feature in sociology, legal theory, and political philosophy. These become relevant

Blockchain technology might turn out to become the ultimate technology of control, able to put all human relationships not into proverbial, but effective, digital chains.

through the practical and material realities of blockchain technologies: the on-chain configurations of protocols, the off-chain governance practices of blockchain communities, and so on. These practices of on- and off-chain governance in turn challenge established political and legal concepts. For instance, our understanding of trust in organizations is challenged by the feature of blockchain being a confidence machine. And similarly, our understanding of measures to enhance legitimacy is challenged by the limitations of coercion, and the role played by exit strategies, in blockchain-based systems.

For those readers in a hurry, here comes the TL;DR ("too long, didn't read"). First, blockchain technology plunges us into a new chapter of the discourse on law and technology. At first, the field was shaped by the emergence of the Internet. The Internet fostered an architectural mode of regulation, according to which code would shape the possibilities of a user's action, thereby encoding equivalences of legal rights, duties, privileges, and prohibitions. In other words, code is law, at least seemingly so. That this *only seemed* to be the case became especially clear with the rise of Internet platforms, which centralized power and thereby both became a target of regulation by the state and sought to instrumentalize software and legal codes for its own ends. Blockchain, by resisting centralization and coercive control, offers an alternative to this rule by code: the rule of code. Just as with the rule of law, this raises important legal and political questions: what procedural and substantive rules should define the rule of code?

Second, blockchain at its core raises the issues of trust and trustlessness. It is meant to do away with trust in third parties, but what does it give us in return? In sociology, we find the helpful distinction between trust—requiring, among others, an addressee and conscious risk-taking—and confidence—requiring, among others, nonaddressable systems and predictability devoid of risk-taking. Blockchain, then, can be described as a confidence machine, where a synthesis of cryptographic primitives, determinative computing, and consensus building produces shared expectations that transactions will be correctly executed. The challenge, however, is to realize that this confidence still depends on a network of actors that requires trust relations. In turn, trust requires the right governance systems and practices to be implemented.

Third, the blockchain confidence machine functions well under normal circumstances but can be significantly challenged by crises. Such a crisis can emerge when a vulnerability in the code is exploited, which in the worst case can lead to an existential threat to a blockchain-based system. When such a threat emerges, private interests in a blockchain network may coalesce and organize themselves as a sovereign power that can decide on whether a state of exception exists and how to resolve it. We can draw lessons about this vulnerability from scholars like Kelsen and Schmitt. Possible responses to the state of exception's vulnerability include strengthening on-chain governance, such as by using PoW instead of segregated witnesses, as well as enhancing off-chain governance, which could involve making rules for the temporary delegation of executive powers to particular actors in a blockchain network.

Fourth, even in normal times blockchain technology is somewhat of a strange regulatory beast because it resists being regulated. As a more potent successor of the claim to "unregulability" of the early Internet, a blockchain network cannot be coerced or simply shut down by any agency, like a state. That is why blockchain proponents have called it an alegal technology, beyond the grasp of the law. Drawing from the legal theory of Lindahl, this claim is warranted to some extent—but not in the same sense as blockchain advocates suggest. Blockchain indeed enables "alegality by design" by configuring actions that may transgress legal boundaries. Yet, states have ways to deal with this alegality, which in some cases involves regulating important intermediaries like exchanges, and in other cases finding functional or regulatory equivalences to shape the legality of blockchain systems.

Fifth, blockchain systems only function when they enjoy legitimacy. Legitimacy, which Buterin called the most important scarce resource of blockchain systems, is needed for a blockchain community to maintain itself and to thrive. It justifies the power vested in the network, which is derived from adherence to specific rules (e.g., those governing blockchain updates), respect for shared beliefs (e.g., immutability), and is usually evidenced by the consent of its participants. Blockchain systems are special in that they allow for relatively easy exit (people can simply leave or fork the blockchain) but depend on the existence of network effects. This raises the importance of voice and loyalty. In most political communities, these aspects are promoted by means of a constitution, a formal document supported by a set of legal norms that justifies the authoritative use of power. Like states, blockchains have constitutions that sit between on-chain (i.e., the protocol) and off-chain governance. Building legitimacy in blockchain systems may be achieved through efforts to draft off-chain constitutions, as some blockchain communities are experimenting with now, but this process entails its own risks.

Policy

Given this TL;DR, there are many challenges of blockchain governance faced by both policymakers and blockchain communities. How can trust be raised through better governance practices? How can blockchain systems be made less vulnerable to states of exception? How can the inherent alegality of blockchain's design be integrated into existing legal systems without undermining decentralization?

How can good governance be formulated and implemented for polycentric blockchain-based systems? And, the most important question, how can the legitimacy of blockchain governance be ensured? Given these myriad questions, different avenues exist for policymakers to respond to the challenges of regulation and governance raised by blockchain technology. On the whole, there are two dominant pathways.

First, governments may pursue "regulation by code," which would follow the dominant approach to Internet governance. Second, governments may pursue a more unconventional but possibly more promising "regulation via governance" approach. Let us look at these two paradigms.

The rise of large Internet platforms has made it apparent that governments can use the codebase of these platforms to implement regulations. Perhaps the most influential case would be the European Union's GDPR. Because this regulation sets standards and limits for the potential configurations of the code developed by centralized organizations, it uses the law-like nature of code to its own advantage. This also allows for code to be audited, to assess whether it incorporates the proper regulatory safeguards, and for organizations to be penalized if these are absent. The centralized nature of players like Google and Meta is a regulatory advantage here because these organizations can function as extensions of the arm of the law. This also becomes apparent, for instance, in criminal investigations, when agencies like the FBI can pressure companies into disclosing users' personal information. Companies, to be sure, still maintain positions of relative autonomy. This was clearly demonstrated by the conflict between Apple and the FBI, where the former refused to provide a "backdoor" into an iPhone's code to give law enforcement access to this phone during a criminal investigation. Yet even though sovereignty in these matters isn't exclusively tied to the state, it is tied to centralized entities and divorced from the user base. X users, for instance, will have to abide either to the rule of law enforced by a state like the United States or to the rule of Elon Musk, who can unilaterally change the codebase (e.g., by taking away the "right" of users to have a blue checkmark).

Blockchain problematizes and challenges this picture. As we saw in chapters 3 and 6, blockchain-based systems introduce the rule of code, which raises the possibility of alegality by design, that is, the potential of these systems to enable acts that transgress legal boundaries. Unlike a centralized platform like X, blockchain-based systems execute code without the possibility of coercion by any single operator. Moreover, they are transnational and (to some extent) decentralized, meaning that shutting down part of a network will not affect the operations of the overall network. This poses significant challenges to regulators, and states have been busy finding ways to reel in the anarchic potential of blockchain-based systems. To be sure, some of these efforts are backed by good reasons, for instance, in cases of cyber criminality and theft. Yet, there is also a risk of throwing out the baby with the bathwater and undoing some of the innovative potentials of blockchain technology.

It is tempting for governments to focus on the low-hanging fruit, which means regulating powerful inter-mediaries in blockchain networks. Indeed, blockchain governance is not purely decentralized but rather functions according to the dynamics of a polycentric system. Many of the stakeholders in a blockchain network are incorporated as legal entities in specific jurisdictions, and are thus susceptible to government regulation. First, mining activities achieved by small businesses or large mining pools are an easy target of state regulation. A case in point is Iran, where commercial mining licenses were initially granted in the years 2019–2020. Later on, however, the political situation changed, and under the surging "climate of fear" in the country, all mining operations were banned to protect against potential energy blackouts. These types of repressive mining regulations can have a negative impact on local businesses, but do not significantly affect the overall functioning of a blockchain, as long as there are sufficient mining activities carried out elsewhere.

Second in line are cryptocurrency exchanges and cus-todian wallets. Because powerful exchanges like Coinbase or Binance control the private keys of their users, they can effectively regulate transactions. Governments have become aware of this crucial function of exchanges, having already implemented KYC, AML, and CTF regulations for the legal operation of crypto exchanges. In the future, this may even lead to a situation where specific addresses or blockchain wallets can be "whitelisted," while others may be "blacklisted." In the wake of the FTX scandal, more comprehensive regulation of cryptocurrency exchanges can be expected. Yet, this regulatory approach also has its limitations, as customers who might not agree with these rules can opt for exchanges operating in jurisdictions with less stringent regulations, or even decentralized exchanges.

Third, even people can become a target of blockchain regulation, most notably developers and end users. The Tornado Cash sanctions, discussed in chapter 6, have put this issue firmly on the agenda. Not only have Tornado Cash developers been prosecuted and imprisoned in the United States and the Netherlands, it has also become illegal for US citizens, residents, and incorporated companies to transact with the Tornado Cash smart contract. Anyone who is caught violating these sanctions will be held criminally liable. Of course, because of the pseudonymous nature of blockchain networks, it is often difficult (but not impossible) to identify who transacts with a smart contract. Another limitation of these regulations is that they are bound to particular jurisdictions and developers can simply move to places with less stringent regulatory regimes. However, when powerful countries like the United States implement these rules, their impact can extend beyond the local jurisdiction, as shown by the fact that the Tornado Cash sanctions have led block producers and exchanges around the world to censor transactions coming from or directed toward these smart contracts.

Thus, states can, albeit indirectly, regulate blockchain-based systems quite effectively. But at what cost? As we discussed in chapter 7, stringent regulation can affect the legitimacy of blockchain-based systems, which may motivate people to exit some systems and look for a better regulatory regime elsewhere. It also raises the question of fairness. Unlike developers working in large companies, blockchain developers working on open-source software can propose changes but have very limited power to decide which changes are incorporated in the codebase. Is it therefore fair to hold a single developer responsible for a change to an open-source project in which pieces of code result from many decisions by many people? There are also structural limitations to personal responsibility as was demonstrated when anonymous users started to send small amounts of Ether from the Tornado Cash smart contract to the wallets of famous public figures, like television host Jimmy Fallon. These actions showed that even though Fallon would be formally liable, his inability to control the transaction directed to his account makes it challenging to attribute responsibility.

Eventually, increasingly stringent regulation that follows the "regulation by code" model may undermine the very innovative potential of blockchain-based systems. First, it may propel the movement toward greater centralization and disincentivize governance experimentation and innovation since communities will experience less autonomy. For instance, people will feel less inclined to support processes of blockchain governance as token holders, as they may fear the burden of liability. And second, it may also have an adverse "race to the bottom" effect because people may choose to exit more strictly regulated systems and look for a new "land" in the buccaneering free haven of the network state, moving the more radical systems even further away from regulatory scrutiny.

The dilemma pictured above forces us to think: does blockchain governance challenge the established ways of regulating technology? If regulation by code proves counterproductive, might blockchain communities, legal and political scholars, and policymakers need to seek out better regulatory environments? Perhaps blockchain raises the core question of regulation under the aegis of cybernetic systems: is regulation still a function of institutional discipline through the law, or is it becoming a function of distributed control? This would mean that blockchain systems and state legislation mutually adapt to one another, functioning as two distinct organisms that need to establish new relationships of coordination and control.

A promising approach to enable this process of mutual adaptation is the establishment of regulatory sandboxes that allow for controlled experimentation with novel governance forms. Think about the federated structure of ancient Greece, where many smaller instances of the polis could experiment with radically new forms of government. A regulatory sandbox implies a scoped regulatory regime, for instance, limited to a particular locality or domain, that allows for greater flexibility and experimentation in the field of governance. It allows for a controlled environment in which people can experiment with new technologies and business models alike, while being exempt from some existing financial regulations and legal requirements. In a sandbox, for instance, initial coin offerings (ICOs) could be made legal provided that they meet specific criteria, inviting practitioners to innovate in order to match these criteria, while giving time for regulations to adapt in order to accommodate these technological innovations.

Regulatory sandboxes are helpful for finding ways to establish "functional equivalence" and "regulatory equivalence" between regulations in the rule of code and those of the rule of law. Functional equivalence establishes the equivalence of two technological artifacts, one that is covered by a legal rule and one that is not yet covered by a legal rule. A relevant example is establishing the equivalence of a paper contract with an electronic contract. Regulatory equivalence means establishing the equivalence of a regulatory regime with a technological implementation of the policy objectives of said regulatory regimes. For instance, DAOs deployed on a public blockchain, having a graphical user interface that enable laypersons to monitor key smart contract variables and transactions, along with plain-language "bylaws" accessible through a public webpage, could be recognized as equivalent to business filings at a corporate registrar. Arguably, this technological implementation can meet the publicity and transparency policy objectives embodied in a corporate governance regime.

As such, regulatory sandboxes can bring about a more constructive form of mutual adjustment between state regulations and blockchain governance. However, given that blockchain communities cannot be forced into this mutual adjustment, conditions should be created that incentivize their engagement. Such an approach, not based on coercion but on incentives, might tame the potential dangers of blockchain governance while not undoing its innovative potential.

An important point of leverage here are the social norms that shape the on- and off-chain governance of blockchain-based systems, which can be influenced by exogenous factors. The strong influence of social norms on governance can be demonstrated by the difference between Bitcoin and Ethereum. While the Bitcoin community emphasizes the value of immutability and the code-is-law principle, the Ethereum community has evolved into fore-grounding distributed consensus, making it easier for the system to flexibly adapt to new circumstances.

Policymakers can try to influence the social norms that codetermine the governance processes of blockchain-based systems by means of incentives. How this works can be illustrated by the case of the Parity bug, as discussed in chapter 5. As a solution to the freezing of over USD 300 million worth of Ether at the time, the Ethereum community decided not to intervene. This decision was partly motivated by the potential exogenous pressures that community members might have faced had intervention occurred. If a standardized procedure for fund recovery had been enabled, some feared, members might have found themselves liable as fiduciaries. Even though it is not clear whether the regulatory environment had a positive impact on the governance process in this particular case, it illustrates the power of states to nudge blockchain communities to adapt new standards, engage in constitutionalizing, and develop governance innovations in particular directions.

Building Cryptopia

The Cambrian explosion of governance structures spurred by blockchain technology is in full swing. It is probable that many new forms of governance will emerge over time as the space progressively matures. But what will the future of blockchain governance look like? Just as Aristotle saw the revolution of governance models eventually consolidate into the unified empire of Alexander the Great, might we expect a consolidation of blockchain governance structures? Or will blockchain technology help us come up with new governance systems that we cannot even conceive of today?

The answers that this book presented to these questions perhaps generate more, rather than less, complexity and uncertainty regarding the possible futures of blockchain governance. But this may also be its core lesson. Blockchain governance is not just a matter of building better rule-of-code systems, with an improved code base and incentive mechanisms. Rather, it also involves grappling with the complex interplay between on- and off-chain governance, trust and confidence building, normal times and emergencies, regulatory oversight and innovative power, dimensions of polycentricity, as well as formal and material constitutional constraints. This is a vast area of investigation, and we are only getting started. What is clear, however, is that building a Cryptopia for realists is urgent and requires collective action, involving crypto communities, scientists, and policymakers.

Alegality
Alegality refers to a state where an action exists in a legal gray area, neither explicitly allowed nor expressly prohibited by existing laws and regulations but by its very existence seeks to change how the distinction between legal and illegal is drawn. In the context of blockchain systems, alegality may pertain to activities or innovations that operate on the edge of legality, often challenging traditional legal frameworks and prompting the need for regulatory clarification.

Bitcoin
Bitcoin is the first cryptocurrency and decentralized payment network created by an anonymous entity known as Satoshi Nakamoto in 2009. It operates on a blockchain, using a proof-of-work consensus mechanism, and serves as a store of value and medium of exchange without the need for intermediaries, central authorities, or physical representation.

Blockchain
A blockchain is a distributed and append-only digital ledger technology that records transactions across a network of computers, ensuring transparency, security, and verifiability. It relies on cryptographic techniques and consensus mechanisms to enable decentralized and tamper-resistant data storage and verification.

Confidence
Confidence refers to the expectations that people hold with regard to how things or systems operate. In the context of blockchain systems, confidence arises from the systems' resiliency and reliability, the immutability and tamper-resistance attributes of the blockchain, and the predictability of its operations grounded in deterministic computation.

Cryptocurrency
Cryptocurrency is a digital form of currency that relies on a blockchain network and cryptographic techniques to secure transactions, control the creation of new units, and verify the transfer of these digital assets, often used as a means of exchange within decentralized ecosystems.

Cypherpunks
Cypherpunks are individuals who advocate for strong cryptography and the use of privacy-enhancing technologies to protect individual freedoms and privacy in the digital age. Their ideas and ideologies have significantly influenced the development of blockchain technology.

Decentralized autonomous organization (DAO)
A decentralized autonomous organization, or DAO, is a blockchain-based organization that operates through code and smart contracts. This structure enables members to make collective decisions and manage shared resources without centralized control, often with voting mechanisms that determine governance decisions and resource allocation.

Ethereum
Ethereum is a blockchain platform and cryptocurrency created by Vitalik Buterin in 2015. It enables the development of smart contracts and decentralized applications on its network, providing a versatile platform for various blockchain-based projects and governance mechanisms beyond simple value transfer.

Hash
In cryptography, a hash is a fixed-length string of characters generated from input data of arbitrary size using a mathematical one-way function called a hash function. This process produces a unique digital fingerprint, or hash value, for each unique set of input data. In the blockchain context, hashes are used to represent the content of a block or transaction, serving as a unique identifier for data integrity and security purposes.

Legitimacy
Legitimacy refers to the perception and acceptance of a governance system's authority and adherence to established rules and principles by its participants and stakeholders. Legitimacy is essential for the long-term sustainability of a blockchain network characterized by low exit costs and significant network effects.

Merkle tree
A Merkle tree is a data structure that organizes and efficiently verifies the integrity of a large dataset by breaking it down into smaller, interconnected

datasets, where each set is represented by a cryptographic hash. This hierarchical structure enables quick and secure verification of specific data elements without needing to process the entire dataset, enhancing data integrity and efficiency in blockchain transactions and validation.

Mining
Mining in the blockchain context refers to the process by which network participants, known as miners, use computational power to solve complex mathematical puzzles and validate transactions on the blockchain. Miners play a crucial role in securing the network and are generally rewarded with cryptocurrency for their efforts.

Polycentricity
Polycentricity refers to a governance system where multiple interdependent centers of decision-making and authority coexist, each trying to influence each other to promote their own interests while nonetheless abiding by a shared set of commonly agreed-upon norms.

Proof of stake (PoS)
Proof of stake, or PoS, is a consensus algorithm employed in blockchain networks where validators, chosen based on the amount of cryptocurrency they hold and are willing to "stake" as collateral, take turns validating transactions and creating new blocks, thereby reducing the energy consumption associated with mining in proof-of-work systems while maintaining a similar level of security.

Proof of work (PoW)
Proof of work, or PoW, is a consensus algorithm used in blockchain networks where participants, known as miners, compete to solve complex mathematical puzzles using computational power to validate and add new blocks to the blockchain, thereby ensuring network security and integrity.

Rule by code
The rule by code, by analogy to the rule by law, refers to the idea that rules encoded in a digital platform can be used to dictate the affordances and constraints for that platform's users. Yet, the operator of the platform is not itself bound by this regulation by code and can therefore instrumentalize the code to further its own interests.

Rule of code

The rule of code, by analogy to the rule of law, refers to the idea that rules encoded in smart contracts and blockchain protocols are autonomously and impartially enforced by the technological infrastructure of the blockchain. This reduces the possibility for any single actor to unilaterally affect the operations of the code unless the code specifically provides for that.

Smart contract

A smart contract is a piece of code deployed on a blockchain network that defines a series of possible actions based on a set of rules and conditions. When predefined conditions are met, the blockchain network automatically executes the smart contract's code in a deterministic manner. Because it does not run on a centralized server, no single actor can influence or terminate the execution of a smart contract.

State of exception

State of exception refers to a legal or political condition where normal legal procedures and civil liberties are temporarily suspended, often during emergencies or crises, granting the government or ruling authority extraordinary powers to address the situation. In a blockchain context, it refers to situations where a blockchain protocol or smart contract does not operate as expected, therefore requiring an extraordinary intervention that violates the protocol rules.

Time stamp

In the blockchain context, a time stamp is a cryptographic record of the exact date and time when a transaction or block is added to the blockchain, ensuring chronological order and data integrity, which is essential for auditability, verification, and consensus in distributed ledger systems.

Trust

Trust involves the expectation that others will act in a manner consistent with one's expectations, commitments, and shared values, even if they have the opportunity not to. Trust constitutes the basis for cooperation, relationships, and social cohesion. It can manifest in various forms, including interpersonal trust, institutional trust, and trust in the functioning of systems and processes.

Chapter 1

1. William Gibson, *Neuromancer* (New York: Ace Books, 1994), 173.

2. Francis Fukuyama, *The End of History and the Last Man* (New York: The Free Press, 1992), ix.

3. Aristotle, *Politics*, ed. and trans. C. D. C. Reeve (Cambridge, MA: Hackett Publishing Company, 1998), 1266b, 38–42.

4. Aristotle, *Politics*, 1267a, 30–35.

5. Aristotle, *Politics*, 1269b, 12–38.

6. Aristotle, *Politics*, 1272b, 21–30.

7. Aristotle, *Politics*, 1274a, 1–10.

8. David Graeber and David Wengrow, *The Dawn of Everything: A New History of Humanity* (London: Penguin, 2022), 9–10.

9. Graeber and Wengrow, *Dawn of Everything*, 4.

10. Maarten Prak, *Citizens without Nations* (Cambridge: Cambridge University Press, 2018), 58.

11. Chris Jennings, *Paradise Now: The Story of American Utopianism* (New York: Random House, 2016), introduction, Kindle.

12. Lewis Mumford, "Utopia, the City and the Machine," *Daedalus* 94, no. 2 (Spring 1965): 283.

13. Gibson, *Neuromancer*.

14. Neal Stephenson, *The Diamond Age, or, Young Lady's Illustrated Primer* (New York: Bantam Books, 1995), 25–28.

15. Ada Palmer, *Too Like the Lightning* (London: Head of Zeus, 2017), 17.

16. Liav Orgad and Rainer Baubock, "Cloud Communities: The Dawn of Global Citizenship?" (RSCAS Working Paper 2018/28, Robert Schuman Centre for Advanced Studies, European University Institute, Fiesole, Italy, 2018), https://hdl.handle.net/1814/55464.

17. Marshall McLuhan, *The Gutenberg Galaxy* (Toronto: University of Toronto Press, 1962).

18. Palmer, *Lightning*, 1.

19. Federica Carugati and Nathan Schneider, "Governance Archeology: Research as Ancestry," *Daedalus* 152, no. 1 (Winter 2023): 245, https://doi.org/10.1162/daed_a_01985.

20. Douglas Rushkoff, *Survival of the Richest: Escape Fantasies of the Tech Billionaires* (New York: W. W. Norton & Company, 2022), chapter 1, Kindle.

21. Sinclair Davidson, Primavera De Filippi, and Jason Potts, "Blockchains and the Economic Institutions of Capitalism," *Journal of Institutional Economics* 14, no. 4 (2018): 640.

22. Vili Lehdonvirta, "The Blockchain Paradox: Why Distributed Ledger Technologies May Do Little to Transform the Economy," Oxford Internet Institute, November 21, 2016, https://www.oii.ox.ac.uk/news-events/news/the-blockchain-paradox-why-distributed-ledger-technologies-may-do-little-to-transform-the-economy/.

23. Iris Chiu, *Regulating the Crypto Economy: Business Transformations and Financialisation* (Oxford: Hart Publishing, 2021), 118; Michèle Finck, *Blockchain Regulation and Governance in Europe* (Cambridge: Cambridge University Press, 2018), 184.

24. Sinclair Davidson and Jason Potts, "Corporate Governance in a Crypto-World" (working paper, May 2022), 11, https://dx.doi.org/10.2139/ssrn.4099906.

25. Chiu, *Crypto Economy*, 114–115.

26. Nathan Schneider, "Cryptoeconomics as a Limitation on Governance," Mirror, August 11, 2022, https://ntnsndr.mirror.xyz/zO27EOn9P_62jVlautpZD5hHB7ycf3Cfc2N6byz6DOk.

Chapter 2

1. Timothy May, "The Crypto-Anarchist Manifesto," in *Crypto Anarchy, Cyberstates, and Pirate Utopias*, ed. Peter Ludlow (Cambridge, MA: MIT Press, 2001), 61.

2. Hannah Arendt, "The Modern Concept of History," *Review of Politics* 20, no. 4 (October 1958): 570–590, https://doi.org/10.1017/S0034670500034227.

3. Hal Finney, "Re: Many Worlds Theory of Immortality," email message to the Everything List, May 9, 2005, https://riceissa.github.io/everything-list-1998-2009/6431.html.

4. Finn Brunton, *Digital Cash: The Unknown History of the Anarchists, Utopians, and Technologists Who Created Cryptocurrency* (Princeton: Princeton University Press, 2020), 55.

5. Max More, "The Extropian Principles," *Extropy Magazine* 6 (1990): 17–18.

6. Max More, "The Extropian Principles, Version 3.0: A Transhumanist Declaration," Extropy Institute, 1998, https://www.mrob.com/pub/religion/extro_prin.html.

7. Raymend Craib, *Adventure Capitalism: A History of Libertarian Exit, from the Era of Decolonization to the Digital Age* (New York: PM Press, 2022), 6.

8. Rushkoff, *Survival of the Richest*, chapter 1.

9. May, "Crypto-Anarchist Manifesto," 61–62.

10. Brunton, *Digital Cash*, 66.

11. Satoshi Nakamoto, "Bitcoin P2P E-Cash Paper," email message to the Cryptography Mailing List, October 31, 2008, 18:10:00 (UTC), https://satoshi.nakamotoinstitute.org/emails/cryptography/1/.

12. Arvind Narayanan and Jeremy Clark, "Bitcoin's Academic Pedigree," *Communications of the ACM* 60, no. 12 (2017): 36–45.

13. Hashing functions are often used to create unique identifiers for digital files. The properties of these functions are such that even the smallest modification to a digital file will generate a completely different and unpredictable hash as an output.

14. Brunton, *Digital Cash*, 166.

15. Alexander Neumueller, "Bitcoin Electricity Consumption: An Improved Assessment," University of Cambridge, Judge Business School Insights, August 31, 2023, https://www.jbs.cam.ac.uk/2023/bitcoin-electricity-consumption/.

16. Ethereum, "The Merge," September 8, 2023, https://ethereum.org/en/roadmap/merge/.

17. Vitalik Buterin, "Ethereum Whitepaper: A Next-Generation Smart Contract and Decentralized Application Platform" (white paper, 2013), https://ethereum.org/en/whitepaper/.

18. Note that Bitcoin also has its own built-in programming language but only as a very limited form of scripting language that is not Turing complete.

19. Primavera De Filippi, Chris Wray, and Giovanni Sileno, "Smart Contracts," *Internet Policy Review* 10, no. 2 (2021): 1–9.

20. Nick Szabo, "Smart Contracts: Building Blocks for Digital Markets," *Extropy: The Journal of Transhumanist Thought* 16, no. 18 (1996): 2–20.

21. Davidson, De Filippi, and Potts, "Economic Institutions of Capitalism," 644.

22. Chiu, *Crypto Economy*, 112.

23. Jaya Klara Brekke and Aron Fischer, "Digital Scarcity," *Internet Policy Review* 10, no. 2 (2021): 1–9.

24. However, it should be noted that all exchanges that allow for swaps between cryptocurrencies and traditional fiat currencies are centralized.

25. Examples include UNI tokens necessary to trade on the Uniswap exchange, PNK tokens enabling people to appeal to the Kleros decentralized

arbitration system, and MANA tokens necessary to buy land on the Decentraland blockchain-based metaverse.

26. Steven Lalley and Glen Weyl, "Quadratic Voting: How Mechanism Design Can Radicalize Democracy," *AEA Papers and Proceedings* 108 (2018): 33–37.

27. Morshed Mannan, "The Promise and Perils of Corporate Governance-by-Design in Blockchain-Based Collectives: The Case of dOrg," in *Co-Operation and Co-Operatives in 21st Century Europe*, ed. Julian Manley, Anthony Webster, and Olga Kuznetsova (Bristol: Bristol University Press, 2023), 78–99.

28. Finck, *Blockchain Regulation*, 198.

29. Nick Szabo, "The Idea of Smart Contracts," *Nick Szabo's Papers and Concise Tutorials* 6, no. 1 (1997): 199.

30. Shermin Voshmgir, "Disrupting Governance with Blockchains and Smart Contracts," *Strategic Change* 26, no. 5 (2017): 499–509.

31. Vitalik Buterin, "DAOs, DACs, DAs and More: An Incomplete Terminology Guide," *Ethereum Foundation Blog*, May 6, 2014, https://blog.ethereum .org/2014/05/06/daos-dacs-das-and-more-an-incomplete-terminology-guide.

32. Samer Hassan and Primavera De Filippi, "Decentralized Autonomous Organization," *Internet Policy Review* 10, no. 2 (2021): 1–10.

33. Davidson, De Filippi, and Potts, "Economic Institutions of Capitalism," 656.

34. Primavera De Filippi, "Citizenship in the Era of Blockchain-Based Virtual Nations," in *Debating Transformations of National Citizenship*, ed. Rainer Baubock (Cham, Switzerland: Springer, 2018), 267–277.

35. Balaji Srinivasan, *The Network State: How to Start a New Country* (self-pub., Amazon Kindle, 2022), 9.

Chapter 3

1. John Perry Barlow, "A Declaration of the Independence of Cyberspace," *Duke Law & Technology Review* 18 (2019): 5.

2. Barlow, "A Declaration of the Independence of Cyberspace," 5.

3. For instance, many online platforms use digital right management systems to restrict access to digital content beyond what is usually provided for by national copyright laws. See, for example, Pamela Samuelson, "DRM {and, or, vs.} the Law," *Communications of the ACM* 46, no. 4 (2003): 41–45.

4. Online platforms have repeatedly violated data protection and privacy laws due to the manner in which they collect user data in order to profile them and/or sell personal information to third-party advertisers (e.g., the Facebook-Cambridge Analytica scandal). See, for example, Jim Isaak and Mina Hanna,

"User Data Privacy: Facebook, Cambridge Analytica, and Privacy Protection," *Computer* 51, no. 8 (2018): 56–59.

5. Lawrence Lessig, *Code and Other Laws of Cyberspace* (New York: Basic Books 1999), 102.

6. Lawrence Lessig, "Code Is Law," *Harvard Magazine* 1 (2000), https://www.harvardmagazine.com/2000/01/code-is-law-html.

7. Vili Lehdonvirta, *Cloud Empires: How Digital Platforms Are Overtaking the State and How We Can Regain Control* (Cambridge MA: MIT Press, 2022), 126.

8. Frank Pasquale, "From Territorial to Functional Sovereignty: The Case of Amazon," Open Democracy, January 5, 2018, https://www.opendemocracy.net/en/digitaliberties/from-territorial-to-functional-sovereignty-case-of-amazon/.

9. Cédric Durand, *Technoféodalisme: Critique de l'économie numérique* (Paris: Zones, 2020), 179.

10. Shoshana Zuboff, *The Age of Surveillance Capitalism: The Fight for a Human Future at the New Frontier of Power* (London: Profile Books, 2019, 4.

11. Evgeny Morozov, "Critique of Technofeudal Reason," *New Left Review* 133/134 (January/April 2022): 89–126.

12. Morozov, "Critique of Techno-Feudal Reason," 97.

13. Tom Bingham, *The Rule of Law* (London: Penguin, 2011), 5.

14. Tom Ginsburg and Tamir Moustafa, *Rule by Law: The Politics of Courts in Authoritarian Regimes* (Cambridge: Cambridge University Press, 2018), 12.

15. David Lyon, "Surveillance, Snowden, and Big Data: Capacities, Consequences, Critique," *Big Data & Society* 1, no. 2 (July–December 2014): 1–13.

16. Michael McGinnis, "Polycentric Governance in Theory and Practice: Dimensions of Aspiration and Practical Limitations" (working paper, Department of Political Science, Indiana University Bloomington, Bloomington, IN, February 2016), 4, https://dx.doi.org/10.2139/ssrn.3812455.

17. Eric Alston et al., "Can Permissionless Blockchains Avoid Governance and the Law?," *Notre Dame Journal on Emerging Technology* 2, no. 1 (March 2021): 1–32.

18. Paul Aligica and Vlad Tarko, "Polycentricity: From Polanyi to Ostrom, and Beyond," *Governance: An International Journal of Policy, Administration, and Institutions* 25, no. 2 (April 2012): 245.

19. Jeremy Waldron, "The Rule of Law and the Importance of Procedure," *Nomos* 50 (2011): 4–5.

20. Primavera de Filippi, Morshed Mannan, and Wessel Reijers, "Blockchain as a Confidence Machine: The Problem of Trust and Challenges of Governance,"

Technology in Society 62 (August 2020): 101284, https://doi.org/10.1016/j.techsoc.2020.101284.

21. Lana Swartz, "Blockchain Dreams: Imagining Techno-Economic Alternatives after Bitcoin," in *Another Economy Is Possible: Culture and Economy in a Time of Crisis*, ed. Manuel Castells (Cambridge, UK: Polity, 2017), 94.

22. Curtis Goldsby and Marvin Hanisch, "The Boon and Bane of Blockchain: Getting the Governance Right," *California Management Review* 64, no. 3 (2022): 141–168.

23. Ashish Rajendra Sai, et al., "Taxonomy of Centralization in Public Blockchain Systems: A Systematic Literature Review" (working paper, September 2020), https://doi.org/10.48550/arXiv.2009.12542.

24. Council Regulation (EU) 2023/1114 on Markets in Crypto-Assets, and amending regulations (EU) no. 1093/2010 and (EU) no. 1095/2010 and directives 2013/36/EU and (EU) 2019/1937, 2023 O.J. (L 150/40) 40 ("MiCA Regulation").

25. MiCA Regulation: recital 12a.

26. Angela Walch, "In Code(rs) We Trust: Software Developers as Fiduciaries in Public Blockchains" in *Regulating Blockchain: Techno-Social and Legal Challenges*, ed. Philipp Hacker et al. (Oxford: Oxford University Press, 2019), 59.

27. *Tulip Trading Limited v. Bitcoin Association for BSV & Ors* [2022] EWHC 667 (Ch) (March 25, 2022), para 75.

28. See the example of the developer arrested in connection with the Tornado Cash case (chapter 6).

29. Evan Miller, "A Tale of Two Regulators: Antitrust Implications of Progressive Decentralization in Blockchain Platforms," *Washington & Lee Law Review Online* 77, no. 2 (2021): 388–409.

30. Mireille Hildebrandt, "Algorithmic Regulation and the Rule of Law," *Philosophical Transactions of the Royal Society A: Mathematical, Physical and Engineering Sciences* 376, no. 2128 (September 2018): 1–11.

31. Karen Yeung, "Regulation by Blockchain: The Emerging Battle for Supremacy between the Code of Law and Code as Law," *Modern Law Review* 82, no. 2 (2019): 210.

32. See, for example, the complaint filed on September 22, 2022 in *Commodity Futures Trading Commission v. Ooki DAO (formerly d/b/a bZx DAO), an Unincorporated Association*, Civil Action No: 3:22-cv-5416 alleging that the governance token-holders of Ooki DAO, as members of an unincorporated association, had violated commodities regulations and were thus jointly and severally liable for this violation.

Chapter 4

1. Herman Melville, *The Confidence Man* (Evanston: Northwestern University Press, 1984), 102.

2. Lana Swartz, "Theorizing the 2017 Blockchain ICO Bubble as a Network Scam," *New Media and Society* 24, no. 7 (2022): 1696. Swartz, in her analysis of ICOs, similarly draws from Melville's work as a "foundational text for understanding scams in modernity."

3. Melville, *The Confidence Man*, 3.

4. Georg Simmel, "The Stranger," in *The Cultural Geography Reader*, ed. Tim Oakes and Patricia L. Price (New York: Routledge, 2008), 311–315.

5. Josh Lauer, *Creditworthy: A History of Consumer Surveillance and Financial Identity in America* (New York: Columbia University Press, 2017), 105.

6. Johannes D. Bergmann, "The Original Confidence Man," *American Quarterly* 21, no. 3 (1969): 561.

7. Bergmann, "The Original Confidence Man," 565.

8. A. P. Martinich, "Two Uses of Thomas Hobbes's Philosophy in Melville's *The Confidence-Man*," *ANQ: A Quarterly Journal of Short Articles, Notes and Reviews* 16, no. 3 (January 2003): 37–40.

9. Frans de Waal, *Primates and Philosophers* (Princeton: Princeton University Press, 2006), 4.

10. Michael Tomasello, *Why We Cooperate* (Cambridge, MA: MIT Press, 2009), xiii.

11. Samuel Bowles and Herbert Gintis, *A Cooperative Species: Human Reciprocity and Its Evolution* (Princeton: Princeton University Press, 2001), 200.

12. Niklas Luhmann, "Familiarity, Confidence, Trust: Problems and Alternatives," in *Trust: Making and Breaking Cooperative Relations*, ed. Diego Gambetta (Oxford: Oxford University Press, 2000), 94–107.

13. Philip Pettit, "The Cunning of Trust," *Philosophy & Public Affairs* 24, no. 3 (1995): 202–225.

14. Russell Hardin, *Trust & Trustworthiness* (New York: Russell Sage Foundation, 2004), 1.

15. Denis J. Roio, "Bitcoin, the End of the Taboo on Money," Dyne.Org Digital Press, April 6, 2013, 1–17.

16. Gili Vidan and Vili Lehdonvirta, "Mine the Gap: Bitcoin and the Maintenance of Trustlessness," *New Media and Society* 21, no. 1 (January 2019): 42–59.

17. Finck, *Blockchain Regulation*, 183.

18. De Filippi, Mannan, and Reijers, "Blockchain as a Confidence Machine."

19. Nick Szabo, "Money, Blockchains, and Social Scalability," Unenumerated, February 9, 2017, http://unenumerated.blogspot.com/2017/02/money-block chains-and-social-scalability.html.

20. Michael Lapointe, "The Edison of the Slot Machines," *Paris Review* February 4, 2020, https://www.theparisreview.org/blog/2020/02/04/the-edison-of -the-slot-machines/.

21. Tim Copeland, "Steem vs Tron: The Rebellion against a Cryptocurrency Empire," Decrypt, August 18, 2020, https://decrypt.co/38050/steem-steemit -tron-justin-sun-cryptocurrency-war.

22. Barbara Guidi, Andrea Michienzi, and Laura Ricci, "Analysis of Witnesses in the Steem Blockchain," *Mobile Networks and Applications* 26, no. 5 (October 2021): 2099–2110.

23. The ninjamined stake refers to an amount of cryptocurrency that was mined by two of the founders of Steem who launched the network earlier than the agreed date. This gave them a head start in mining the native tokens, which would represent 30 percent of the network's total token supply at a later point, when Justin Sun bought the stake for USD 8 million.

24. Copeland, "Steem vs Tron."

25. Christopher Harland-Dunaway, "The Many Escapes of Justin Sun," The Verge, March 9, 2022, https://www.theverge.com/c/22947663/justin-sun -tron-cryptocurrency-poloniex.

Chapter 5

1. Carl Schmitt, *Political Theology: Four Chapters on the Concept of Sovereignty* (Chicago: University of Chicago Press, 2005), 15.

2. John M. Coetzee, *Waiting for the Barbarians* (New York: Penguin Books, 1999), 4.

3. C. P. Cavafy, *Collected Poems*, ed. George Savidis, trans. Edmund Keeley and Philip Sherrard, rev. ed. (Princeton: Princeton University Press, 1992), 20.

4. Coetzee, *Waiting for the Barbarians*, 177.

5. Carl Schmitt was and remains controversial because of his involvement in the Nazi party as a prominent and unapologetic member, as well as the resonance between his political and legal ideas and the authoritarian politics of Nazi Germany.

6. Schmitt, *Political Theology*, 5.

7. Nassim N. Taleb, *The Black Swan: The Impact of the Highly Improbable* (London: Random House, 2017), xviii.

8. Hans Kelsen, *Pure Theory of Law* (Clark, NJ: The Lawbook Exchange, 2005), 3.

9. Schmitt, *Political Theology*, 48.

10. Quinn Dupont, "Experiments in Algorithmic Governance: A History and Ethnography of 'The DAO,' a Failed Decentralized Autonomous Organization," in *Bitcoin and Beyond*, ed. Malcolm Campbell-Verduyn (New York: Routledge, 2017), 157–177.

11. Kelsen, *Pure Theory of Law*, 194.

12. Kelsen, *Pure Theory of Law*, 202.

13. Francis Ghilès, "France's Permanent State of Emergency." *Barcelona Center for International Affairs* 502 (2017): 1–2.

14. David Dyzenhaus, *Legality and Legitimacy: Carl Schmitt, Hans Kelsen and Herman Heller in Weimar* (Oxford: Oxford University Press, 1997), 5.

15. Coetzee, *Waiting for the Barbarians*, 7.

16. David Dyzenhaus, "Now the Machine Runs Itself," *Cardozo Law Review* 16, no. 1 (1994): 10.

17. Vitalik Buterin, "Critical Update Re: DAO Vulnerability," *Ethereum Foundation Blog*, June 17, 2016, https://blog.ethereum.org/2016/06/17/critical -update-re-dao-vulnerability.

18. The Attacker, "An Open Letter," https://pastebin.com/CcGUBgDG.

19. Clinton Rossiter, *Constitutional Dictatorship: Crisis Government in the Modern Democracies* (New York: Routledge, 1948), 290.

Chapter 6

1. Quoted from Paul Eltzbacher, *Anarchism* (New York: Benjamin R. Tucker, 1908), 129.

2. Srinivasan, *The Network State*, 9.

3. Srinivasan, *The Network State*, 234.

4. Gavin Wood. "Allegality: Systems That Can't Care," YouTube video, 26:30, May 14, 2015, https://www.youtube.com/watch?v=Zh9BxYTSrGU.

5. Laura Shin, *The Cryptopians: Idealism, Greed, Lies, and the Making of the First Big Cryptocurrency Craze* (New York: PublicAffairs, 2022), chapter 5, Kindle.

6. Vanja Hamzić, "Alegality: Outside and Beyond the Legal Logic of Late Capitalism," in *Neoliberal Legality: Understanding the Role of Law in the Neoliberal Project*, ed. Honor Brabazon (Abingdon: Routledge, 2017), 191.

7. Hans Lindahl, "We and Cyberlaw: The Spatial Unity of Constitutional Orders," *Indiana Journal of Global Legal Studies* 20, no. 2 (2013): 730.

8. Hans Lindahl, *Authority and the Globalisation of Inclusion and Exclusion* (Cambridge, UK: Cambridge University Press, 2018), 60.

9. Hans Lindahl, "A-Legality: Postnationalism and the Question of Legal Boundaries," *Modern Law Review* 73, no. 1 (2010): 35.

10. Lindahl, *Authority*, 143–144.

11. Hans Lindahl, *Fault Lines of Globalization: Legal Order and the Politics of A-Legality* (Oxford: Oxford University Press, 2013), 21.

12. Carys Hughes, "Action between the Legal and the Illegal: A-Legality as a Political–Legal Strategy," *Social & Legal Studies* 28, no. 4 (2019): 472.

13. Hans Lindahl, "Inside and Outside Global Law," *Sydney Law Review* 41, no. 1 (2019): 18.

14. Lindahl, "Inside and Outside," 22.

15. Alexander Behrens, "'Not Your Keys; Not Your Coins' Enshrined in US Case Law, Says Lawyer," Decrypt, August 23, 2020, https://decrypt.co/39574/not-your-keys-not-your-coins-enshrined-in-us-case-law-says-lawyer.

16. Langdon Winner, "Do Artifacts Have Politics?" *Daedalus* 109, no. 1 (Winter 1980): 123.

17. Primavera de Filippi, Morshed Mannan, and Wessel Reijers, "The Alegality of Blockchain Technology," *Policy and Society* 41, no. 3 (2022): 359.

18. Tornado Cash, "Tornado.cash Is Finally Trustless!" Medium, May 20, 2022, https://tornado-cash.medium.com/tornado-cash-is-finally-trustless-a6e119c1d1c2.

19. *Joseph van Loon v. Department of Treasury*, 1:23-CV-312-RP (W.D.Tex. Aug. 17, 2023).

20. Jerry Brito and Peter van Valkenburgh, "Analysis: What Is and What Is Not a Sanctionable Entity in the Tornado Cash Case," Coin Center, August 15, 2022, https://www.coincenter.org/analysis-what-is-and-what-is-not-a-sanctionable-entity-in-the-tornado-cash-case/.

21. Henry Farrell and Bruce Schneier, "Tornado Cash Is Not Free Speech. It Is a Golem," Lawfare, October 13, 2022, https://www.lawfaremedia.org/article/tornado-cash-not-free-speech-its-golem.

22. Eltzbacher, *Anarchism*, 129.

Chapter 7

1. Vitalik Buterin, "The Most Important Scarce Resource Is Legitimacy," Vitalik.ca, March 23, 2021, https://web.archive.org/web/20230324211049/https://vitalik.ca/general/2021/03/23/legitimacy.html.

2. Vitalik Buterin, "The Most Important Scarce Resource Is Legitimacy."

3. Roger Cotterrell, *Law's Community: Legal Theory in Sociological Perspective* (Oxford: Oxford University Press, 1997), 136.

4. Dyzenhaus, *Legality and Legitimacy*, 1–2.

5. Dyzenhaus, *Legality and Legitimacy*, 246, 254.

6. Mikolaj Barczentewicz, Alex Sarch, and Natasha Vasan, "Blockchain Transaction Ordering as Market Manipulation," *Ohio State Technology Law Journal* 20 (forthcoming), 6, http://dx.doi.org/10.2139/ssrn.4187752.

7. Barczentewicz, Sarch, and Vasan, "Blockchain Transaction Ordering," 47.

8. Ross Mittiga, "Political Legitimacy, Authoritarianism, and Climate Change," *American Political Science Review* 116, no. 3 (August 2022): 1001.

9. Allen Buchanan, "Political Legitimacy and Democracy," *Ethics* 112, no. 4 (2002): 703.

10. Mittiga, "Political Legitimacy," 1001–1002.

11. De Filippi, Mannan, and Reijers, "Confidence Machine," 6.

12. De Filippi, Mannan, and Reijers, "Confidence Machine," 12.

13. Buchanan, "Political Legitimacy," 703.

14. Nathan Schneider, "How We Can Encode Human Rights in the Blockchain," Noema, June 7, 2022, https://www.noemamag.com/how-we-can-encode -human-rights-in-the-blockchain/.

15. Ellie Rennie, "Climate Change and the Legitimacy of Bitcoin" (working paper, January 2023), 6–9, https://dx.doi.org/10.2139/ssrn.3961105.

16. Adam French, "Regenerative Web 3—The Landscape, Opportunities, and Entry Point," *Gitcoin Blog*, January 16, 2023, https://www.gitcoin.co/blog /regenerative-web-3-the-landscape-opportunities-and-entry-points.

17. Greg Ahlstrand, "New York Imposes 2-Year Moratorium on New Proof-of-Work Mining after Gov. Hochul Signs Bill," CoinDesk, November 23, 2022, https://www.coindesk.com/policy/2022/11/23/new-york-imposes-2-year -moratorium-on-new-proof-of-work-mining-after-governor-hochul-signs-bill -into-law/.

18. Vivien Schmidt, *Europe's Crisis of Legitimacy: Governing by Rules and Ruling by Numbers in the Eurozone* (Oxford: Oxford University Press, 2020), 25.

19. Julia Black, "Constructing and Contesting Legitimacy and Accountability in Polycentric Regulatory Regimes," *Regulation & Governance* 2, no. 2 (June 2008): 144.

20. Shruti Rajagopalan, "Blockchain and Buchanan: Code as Constitution," in *James M. Buchanan: A Theorist of Political Economy and Social Philosophy*, ed. Richard Wagner (Cham, Switzerland: Palgrave Macmillan, 2018), 377.

21. Russell Hardin, "Why a Constitution?," in *Social and Political Foundations of Constitutions*, ed. Denis J. Galligan and Mila Versteeg (Cambridge: Cambridge University Press, 2013), 51.

22. Tobias Mahler, *Generic Top-Level Domains: A Study of Transnational Private Regulation* (Cheltenham: Edward Elgar, 2019), 40.

23. Angelo Golia, "The Transformative Potential of Meta's Oversight Board: Strategic Litigation within the Digital Constitution?" *Indiana Journal of Global Legal Studies* 30 (forthcoming), 9, https://ssrn.com/abstract=4401086.

24. Giovanni de Gregorio, "Digital Constitutionalism across the Atlantic," *Global Constitutionalism* 11, no. 2 (2022): 317; Nicolas Suzor, "Digital Constitutionalism: Using the Rule of Law to Evaluate the Legitimacy of Governance by Platforms," *Social Media + Society* 4, no. 3 (July–September 2018): 5–7.

25. Eric Alston, "Constitutions and Blockchains: Competitive Governance of Fundamental Rule Sets," *Journal of Law, Technology & the Internet* 11, no. 5 (2020): 134; Rajagopalan, "Blockchain and Buchanan," 366–367.

26. Alston, "Constitutions and Blockhains," 151.

27. Ferdinand Lassalle, "On the Essence of Constitutions," *Fourth International* 3, no. 1 (1942): 25–31, https://www.marxists.org/history/etol/news pape/fi/vol03/no01/lassalle.htm.

28. ENS, "ENS DAO Constitution," ENS Documentation, accessed December 22, 2023, https://docs.ens.domains/v/governance/ens-dao-constitution.

29. Joshua Tan et al., "Constitutions of Web3" (working paper, September 2023), https://constitutions.metagov.org/article.

30. Eric Alston et al., "Blockchain Networks as Constitutional and Competitive Polycentric Orders," *Journal of Institutional Economics* 18, no. 5 (October 2022): 721.

Chapter 8

1. Jean-Jacques Rousseau, *The Social Contract* (Hertfordshire: Wordsworth Editions Limited, 1998), 5.

2. Hannu Rajaniemi, "Unchained: A Story of Love, Loss, and Blockchain," *MIT Technology Review*, April 25, 2018, https://www.technologyreview.com/2018/04/25/143469/unchained-a-story-of-love-loss-and-blockchain/.

BIBLIOGRAPHY

Ahlstrand, Greg. "New York Imposes 2-Year Moratorium on New Proof-of-Work Mining after Gov. Hochul Signs Bill." CoinDesk, November 23, 2022. https://www.coindesk.com/policy/2022/11/23/new-york-imposes-2-year -moratorium-on-new-proof-of-work-mining-after-governor-hochul-signs-bill -into-law/.

Aligica, Paul, and Vlad Tarko. "Polycentricity: From Polanyi to Ostrom, and Beyond." *Governance: An International Journal of Policy, Administration, and Institutions* 25, no. 2 (April 2012): 237–262.

Alston, Eric. "Constitutions and Blockchains: Competitive Governance of Fundamental Rule Sets." *Journal of Law, Technology & the Internet* 11, no. 5 (2020): 131–171.

Alston, Eric, Wilson Law, Ilia Murtazashvili, and Martin Weiss. "Can Permissionless Blockchains Avoid Governance and the Law?" *Notre Dame Journal on Emerging Technology* 2, no. 1 (March 2021): 1–32.

Alston, Eric, Wilson Law, Ilia Murtazashvili, and Martin Weiss. "Blockchain Networks as Constitutional and Competitive Polycentric Orders." *Journal of Institutional Economics* 18, no. 5 (October 2022): 707–723.

Arendt, Hannah. "The Modern Concept of History." *Review of Politics* 20, no. 4 (October 1958): 570–590.

Aristotle. *Politics*. Edited and translated by C. D. C. Reeve. Cambridge, MA: Hackett Publishing Company, 1998.

The Attacker. "An Open Letter." https://pastebin.com/CcGUBgDG.

Bakunin, Mikhail. "Man, Society and Freedom." In *Bakunin on Anarchy: Selected Works by the Activist-Founder of World*, edited by Sam Dolgoff, 234–242. New York: Vintage Book, 1971.

Barczentewicz, Mikolaj, Alex Sarch, and Natasha Vasan. "Blockchain Transaction Ordering as Market Manipulation." *Ohio State Technology Law Journal* 20 (forthcoming): 6.

Barlow, John Perry. "A Declaration of the Independence of Cyberspace." *Duke Law & Technology Review* 18 (2019): 5–7.

Behrens, Alexander. "'Not Your Keys; Not Your Coins' Enshrined in US Case Law, Says Lawyer." Decrypt, August 23, 2020. https://decrypt.co/39574/not-your-keys-not-your-coins-enshrined-in-us-case-law-says-lawyer.

Bergmann, Johannes D. "The Original Confidence Man." *American Quarterly* 21, no. 3 (1969): 560–577.

Bingham, Tom. *The Rule of Law*. London: Penguin, 2011.

Black, Julia. "Constructing and Contesting Legitimacy and Accountability in Polycentric Regulatory Regimes." *Regulation & Governance* 2, no. 2 (June 2008): 137–164.

Bowles, Samuel, and Herbert Gintis. *A Cooperative Species: Human Reciprocity and Its Evolution*. Princeton: Princeton University Press, 2001.

Brekke, Jaya Klara, and Aron Fischer. "Digital Scarcity." *Internet Policy Review* 10, no. 2 (2021): 1–9.

Brito, Jerry, and van Valkenburgh, Peter, "Analysis: What Is and What Is Not a Sanctionable Entity in the Tornado Cash Case." Coin Center, August 15, 2022. https://www.coincenter.org/analysis-what-is-and-what-is-not-a-sanctionable-entity-in-the-tornado-cash-case/.

Brunton, Finn. *Digital Cash: The Unknown History of the Anarchists, Utopians, and Technologists Who Created Cryptocurrency*. Princeton: Princeton University Press, 2020.

Buchanan, Allen. "Political Legitimacy and Democracy." *Ethics* 112, no. 4 (2002): 689–719.

Buterin, Vitalik. "Critical Update Re: DAO Vulnerability." *Ethereum Foundation Blog*, June 17, 2016. https://blog.ethereum.org/2016/06/17/critical-update-re-dao-vulnerability.

Buterin, Vitalik. "DAOs, DACs, DAs and More: An Incomplete Terminology Guide." *Ethereum Foundation Blog*, May 6, 2014. https://blog.ethereum.org/2014/05/06/daos-dacs-das-and-more-an-incomplete-terminology-guide.

Buterin, Vitalik. "Ethereum Whitepaper: A Next-Generation Smart Contract and Decentralized Application Platform." White paper, 2013. https://ethereum.org/en/whitepaper/.

Buterin, Vitalik. "The Most Important Scarce Resource Is Legitimacy." Vitalik.ca, March 23, 2021. https://web.archive.org/web/20230324211049/https://vitalik.ca/general/2021/03/23/legitimacy.html.

Carugati, Federica, and Nathan Schneider. "Governance Archeology: Research as Ancestry." *Daedalus* 152, no. 1 (Winter 2023): 245–257. https://doi.org/10.1162/daed_a_01985.

Cavafy, Constantine P. *Collected Poems*. Edited by George Savidis and translated by Edmund Keeley and Philip Sherrard. Rev. ed. Princeton: Princeton University Press, 1992.

Chio, Ka. "Rule of Law or Rule by Law? A Brief Analysis of China's Legal System." *International Relations Journal* 33 (Spring 2014): 29–43.

Chiu, Iris. *Regulating the Crypto Economy: Business Transformations and Financialisation*. Oxford: Hart Publishing, 2021.

Coetzee, John M. *Waiting for the Barbarians*. New York: Penguin Books, 1999.

Copeland, Tim. "Steem vs Tron: The Rebellion against a Cryptocurrency Empire." Decrypt, August 18, 2020. https://decrypt.co/38050/steem-steemit-tron-justin-sun-cryptocurrency-war.

Cotterrell, Roger. *Law's Community: Legal Theory in Sociological Perspective*. Oxford: Oxford University Press, 1997.

Craib, Raymond. *Adventure Capitalism: A History of Libertarian Exit, from the Era of Decolonization to the Digital Age*. New York: PM Press, 2022.

Davidson, Sinclair, Primavera De Filippi, and Jason Potts. "Blockchains and the Economic Institutions of Capitalism." *Journal of Institutional Economics* 14, no. 4 (2018): 639–658.

Davidson, Sinclair, and Jason Potts. "Corporate Governance in a Crypto-World." Working paper, May 2022. https://dx.doi.org/10.2139/ssrn.4099906.

De Filippi, Primavera, and Benjamin Loveluck. "The Invisible Politics of Bitcoin: Governance Crisis of a Decentralized Infrastructure." *Internet Policy Review* 5, no. 4 (2016). https://papers.ssrn.com/sol3/papers.cfm?abstract_id=2852691.

De Filippi, Primavera. "Citizenship in the Era of Blockchain-Based Virtual Nations." In *Debating Transformations of National Citizenship*, edited by Rainer Baubock, 267–278 Cham, Switzerland: Springer, 2018.

De Filippi, Primavera, Morshed Mannan, and Wessel Reijers. "Blockchain as a Confidence Machine: The Problem of Trust and Challenges of Governance." *Technology in Society* 62 (August 2020): 101284. https://doi.org/10.1016/j.techsoc.2020.101284.

De Filippi, Primavera, Chris Wray, and Giovanni Sileno. "Smart Contracts." *Internet Policy Review* 10, no. 2 (2021): 1–9.

De Filippi, Primavera, Morshed Mannan, and Wessel Reijers. "The Alegality of Blockchain Technology." *Policy and Society* 41, no. 3 (2022): 358–372.

De Waal, Frans. *Primates and Philosophers*. Princeton: Princeton University Press, 2006.

Dupont, Quinn. "Experiments in Algorithmic Governance: A History and Ethnography of 'The DAO,' a Failed Decentralized Autonomous Organization." In *Bitcoin and Beyond*, edited by Malcolm Campbell-Verduyn, 157–177. New York: Routledge, 2017.

Durand, Cédric. *Technoféodalisme: Critique de l'économie numérique*. Paris: Zones, 2020.

Dyzenhaus, David. *Legality and Legitimacy: Carl Schmitt, Hans Kelsen and Herman Heller in Weimar*. Oxford: Oxford University Press, 1997.

Dyzenhaus, David. "Now the Machine Runs Itself." *Cardozo Law Review* 16, no. 1 (1994): 1–19.

Eltzbacher, Paul. *Anarchism*. New York: Benjamin R. Tucker, 1908.

Ethereum. "The Merge." September 8, 2023. https://ethereum.org/en/roadmap/merge/.

Farrell, Henry, and Bruce Schneier. "Tornado Cash Is Not Free Speech. It Is a Golem." Lawfare, October 13, 2022. https://www.lawfaremedia.org/article/tornado-cash-not-free-speech-its-golem.

Finck, Michèle. *Blockchain Regulation and Governance in Europe*. Cambridge: Cambridge University Press, 2018.

Finney, Hal. "Re: Many Worlds Theory of Immortality." Email Message to Extropians Mailing List, May 9, 2005. https://riceissa.github.io/everything-list-1998-2009/6431.html.

French, Adam. "Regenerative Web 3—The Landscape, Opportunities, and Entry Point." *Gitcoin Blog*, January 16, 2023. https://www.gitcoin.co/blog/regenerative-web-3-the-landscape-opportunities-and-entry-points.

Fukuyama, Francis. *The End of History and the Last Man*. New York: The Free Press, 1992.

Gambetta, Diego. "Can We Trust Trust?" In *Trust: Making and Breaking Cooperative Relations*, edited by Diego Gambetta, 213–237. Oxford: University of Oxford Press, 2000.

Gibson, William. *Neuromancer*. New York: Ace Books, 1994.

Ginsburg, Tom, and Tamir Moustafa. *Rule by Law: The Politics of Courts in Authoritarian Regimes*. Cambridge: Cambridge University Press, 2018.

Ghilès, Francis. "France's Permanent State of Emergency." *Barcelona Center for International Affairs* 502 (2017): 1–2.

GlobalData. "Bitcoin Market Capitalisation History." GlobalData: Data & Insights, September 15, 2023. https://www.globaldata.com/data-insights/finan cial-services/bitcoins-market-capitalization-history.

Goldsby, Curtis, and Marvin Hanisch. "The Boon and Bane of Blockchain: Getting the Governance Right." *California Management Review* 64, no. 3 (2022): 141–168.

Golia, Angelo. "The Transformative Potential of Meta's Oversight Board: Strategic Litigation within the Digital Constitution?" *Indiana Journal of Global Legal Studies* 30 (forthcoming). https://ssrn.com/abstract=4401086.

Graeber, David, and David Wengrow. *The Dawn of Everything: A New History of Humanity*. London: Penguin, 2022.

Gregorio, Giovanni de. "Digital Constitutionalism across the Atlantic," *Global Constitutionalism* 11, no. 2 (2022): 297–324.

Guidi, Barbara, Andrea Michienzi, and Laura Ricci. "Analysis of Witnesses in the Steem Blockchain." *Mobile Networks and Applications* 26, no. 5 (October 2021): 2099–2110. https://doi.org/10.1007/s11036-021-01749-x.

Hamzić, Vanja. "Alegality: Outside and Beyond the Legal Logic of Late Capitalism." In *Neoliberal Legality: Understanding the Role of Law in the Neoliberal Project*, edited by Honor Brabazon, 190–209. Abingdon: Routledge, 2017.

Hardin, Russell. *Trust & Trustworthiness*. New York: Russell Sage Foundation, 2004.

Hardin, Russell. "Why a Constitution?" In *Social and Political Foundations of Constitutions*, edited by Denis J. Galligan and Mila Versteeg, 51–72. Cambridge: Cambridge University Press, 2013.

Harland-Dunaway, Christopher. "The Many Escapes of Justin Sun." The Verge, March 9, 2022. https://www.theverge.com/c/22947663/justin-sun-tron-cryptocurrency-poloniex.

Hassan, Samer, and Primavera De Filippi. "Decentralized Autonomous Organization." *Internet Policy Review* 10, no. 2 (2021): 1–10. https://policyreview.info/glossary/DAO.

Heinlein, Robert. *Double Star*. New York: Doubleday & Co., 1956.

Hildebrandt, Mireille. "Algorithmic Regulation and the Rule of Law." *Philosophical Transactions of the Royal Society A: Mathematical, Physical and Engineering Sciences* 376, no. 2128 (September 2018): 1–11.

Hughes, Carys. "Action between the Legal and the Illegal: A-Legality as a Political–Legal Strategy." *Social & Legal Studies* 28, no. 4 (2019): 470–492. https://doi.org/10.1177/0964663918791009.

Isaak, Jim, and Mina J. Hanna. "User Data Privacy: Facebook, Cambridge Analytica, and Privacy Protection." *Computer* 51, no. 8 (2018): 56–59.

Jennings, Chris. *Paradise Now: The Story of American Utopianism*. New York: Random House, 2016. Kindle.

Kelsen, Hans. *Pure Theory of Law*. Clark: The Lawbook Exchange, 2005.

Lalley, Steven, and Glen Weyl. "Quadratic Voting: How Mechanism Design Can Radicalize Democracy." *AEA Papers and Proceedings* 108 (2018): 33–37.

Lapointe, Michael. "The Edison of the Slot Machines." *Paris Review*, February 4, 2020. https://www.theparisreview.org/blog/2020/02/04/the-edison-of-the-slot-machines/.

Lassalle, Ferdinand. "On the Essence of Constitutions." *Fourth International* 3, no. 1 (1942): 25–31. https://www.marxists.org/history/etol/newspape/fi/vol03/no01/lassalle.htm.

Lauer, Josh. *Creditworthy: A History of Consumer Surveillance and Financial Identity in America*. New York: Columbia University Press, 2017.

Lehdonvirta, Vili. *Cloud Empires: How Digital Platforms Are Overtaking the State and How We Can Regain Control*. Cambridge MA: MIT Press, 2022.

Lehdonvirta, Vili. "The Blockchain Paradox: Why Distributed Ledger Technologies May Do Little to Transform the Economy." Oxford Internet Institute

Blog, November 21, 2016. https://www.oii.ox.ac.uk/news-events/news/the
-blockchain-paradox-why-distributed-ledger-technologies-may-do-little-to
-transform-the-economy/.

Lessig, Lawrence. *Code and Other Laws of Cyberspace*. New York: Basic Books, 1999.

Lessig, Lawrence. "Code Is Law." *Harvard Magazine* 1 (2000).

Lindahl, Hans. "A-Legality: Postnationalism and the Question of Legal Boundaries." *Modern Law Review* 73, no. 1 (2010): 30–56.

Lindahl, Hans. *Fault Lines of Globalization: Legal Order and the Politics of A-Legality*. Oxford: Oxford University Press, 2013.

Lindahl, Hans. "We and Cyberlaw: The Spatial Unity of Constitutional Orders." *Indiana Journal of Global Legal Studies* 20, no. 2 (2013): 697–730.

Lindahl, Hans. *Authority and the Globalisation of Inclusion and Exclusion*. Cambridge, UK: Cambridge University Press, 2018.

Lindahl, Hans. "Inside and Outside Global Law." *Sydney Law Review* 41, no. 1 (2019): 1–34.

Luhmann, Niklas. "Familiarity, Confidence, Trust: Problems and Alternatives." In *Trust: Making and Breaking Cooperative Relations*, edited by Diego Gambetta, 94–107. Oxford: Oxford University Press, 2000.

Lyon, David. "Surveillance, Snowden, and Big Data: Capacities, Consequences, Critique." *Big Data & Society* 1, no. 2 (July–December 2014): 1–13.

Mahler, Tobias. *Generic Top-Level Domains: A Study of Transnational Private Regulation*. Cheltenham: Edward Elgar, 2019.

Mannan, Morshed. "The Promise and Perils of Corporate Governance-by-Design in Blockchain-Based Collectives: The Case of dOrg." In *Co-Operation and Co-Operatives in 21st Century Europe*, edited by Julian Manley, Anthony Webster, and Olga Kuznetsova, 78–99. Bristol: Bristol University Press, 2023.

Martinich, Aloysius P. "Two Uses of Thomas Hobbes's Philosophy in Melville's *The Confidence-Man*." *ANQ: A Quarterly Journal of Short Articles, Notes and Reviews* 16, no. 3 (January 2003): 37–40. https://doi.org/10.1080/08957690309598214.

May, Timothy. "The Crypto-Anarchist Manifesto." In *Crypto Anarchy, Cyberstates, and Pirate Utopias*, edited by Peter Ludlow, 61–63. Cambridge, MA: MIT Press, 2001.

McGinnis, Michael. "Polycentric Governance in Theory and Practice: Dimensions of Aspiration and Practical Limitations." Working paper, Department of Political Science, Indiana University Bloomington, Bloomington, IN, February 2016. https://dx.doi.org/10.2139/ssrn.3812455.

McLuhan, Marshall. *The Gutenberg Galaxy*. Toronto: University of Toronto Press, 1962.

Melville, Herman. *The Confidence Man*. Evanston: Northwestern University Press, 1984.

Miller, Evan. "A Tale of Two Regulators: Antitrust Implications of Progressive Decentralization in Blockchain Platforms." *Washington & Lee Law Review Online* 77, no. 2 (2021): 386–409.

Mitchell, Lawrence. "Trust and the Overlapping Consensus." *Columbia Law Review* 94, no. 6 (1994): 1918–1935.

Mittiga, Ross. "Political Legitimacy, Authoritarianism, and Climate Change." *American Political Science Review* 116, no. 3 (August 2022): 998–1011.

More, Max. "The Extropian Principles" *Extropy Magazine* 6 (1990): 17–18.

More, Max. "The Extropian Principles, Version 3.0: A Transhumanist Declaration." Extropy Institute, 1998. https://www.mrob.com/pub/religion/extro _prin.html.

Morozov, Evgeny. "Critique of Techno-Feudal Reason." *New Left Review* 133/134 (January/April 2022): 89–126.

Mumford, Lewis. "Utopia, the City and the Machine." *Daedalus* 94, no. 2 (Spring 1965): 271–292.

Narayanan, Arvind, and Jeremy Clark. "Bitcoin's Academic Pedigree." *Communications of the ACM* 60, no. 12 (2017): 36–45.

Neumueller, Alexander. "Bitcoin Electricity Consumption: An Improved Assessment." University of Cambridge, Judge Business School Insights, August 31, 2023. https://www.jbs.cam.ac.uk/2023/bitcoin-electricity-consumption/.

Orgad, Liav, and Rainer Baubock. "Cloud Communities: The Dawn of Global Citizenship?" RSCAS Working Paper 2018/28, Robert Schuman Centre for Advanced Studies, European University Institute, Fiesole, Italy, 2018. https://hdl .handle.net/1814/55464.

Palmer, Ada. *Too Like the Lightning*. London: Head of Zeus, 2017.

Pasquale, Frank. "From Territorial to Functional Sovereignty: The Case of Amazon." Open Democracy, January 5, 2018. https://www.opendemocracy.net/en/digitaliberties/from-territorial-to-functional-sovereignty-case-of-amazon/.

Pettit, Philip. "The Cunning of Trust." *Philosophy & Public Affairs* 24, no. 3 (1995): 202–225.

Prak, Maarten. *Citizens without Nations*. Cambridge: Cambridge University Press, 2018.

Rajagopalan, Shruti. "Blockchain and Buchanan: Code as Constitution." In *James M. Buchanan: A Theorist of Political Economy and Social Philosophy*, edited by Richard Wagner, 359–381. Cham, Switzerland: Palgrave Macmillan, 2018.

Rajaniemia, Hannu. "Unchained: A Story of Love, Loss, and Blockchain." *MIT Technology Review*, April 25, 2018. https://www.technologyreview.com/2018/04/25/143469/unchained-a-story-of-love-loss-and-blockchain/.

Rajendra Sai, Ashish, Jim Buckley, Brian Fitzgerald, and Andrew Le Gear. "Taxonomy of Centralization in Public Blockchain Systems: A Systematic Literature Review." Working paper, September 26, 2020. https://doi.org/10.48550/arXiv.2009.12542.

Rennie, Ellie. "Climate Change and the Legitimacy of Bitcoin." Working paper, January 2023. https://dx.doi.org/10.2139/ssrn.3961105.

Roio, Denis J. "Bitcoin, the End of the Taboo on Money." Dyne.Org Digital Press, April 6, 2013, 1–17. https://median.newmediacaucus.org/isea2012-machine-wilderness/bitcom-the-end-of-the-taboo-on-money/.

Rossiter, Clinton. *Constitutional Dictatorship: Crisis Government in the Modern Democracies*. New York: Routledge, 1948.

Rousseau, Jean-Jacques. *The Social Contract*. Hertfordshire: Wordsworth Editions Limited, 1998.

Rushkoff, Douglas. *Survival of the Richest: Escape Fantasies of the Tech Billionaires*. New York: W. W. Norton & Company, 2022. Kindle.

Samuelson, Pamela. "DRM {and, or, vs.} the Law." *Communications of the ACM* 46, no. 4 (2003): 41–45.

Schmidt, Vivien. *Europe's Crisis of Legitimacy: Governing by Rules and Ruling by Numbers in the Eurozone*. Oxford: Oxford University Press, 2020.

Schmitt, Carl. Political Theology: Four Chapters on the Concept of Sovereignty. Chicago: University of Chicago Press, 2005.

Schneider, Nathan. "How We Can Encode Human Rights in the Blockchain." Noema, June 7, 2022. https://www.noemamag.com/how-we-can-encode -human-rights-in-the-blockchain/.

Schneider, Nathan. "Cryptoeconomics as a Limitation on Governance." Mirror, August 11, 2022. https://ntnsndr.mirror.xyz/zO27EOn9P_62jVlautpZD5hH B7ycf3Cfc2N6byz6DOk.

Schochet, Gordon J. "Thomas Hobbes on the Family and the State of Nature." *Political Science Quarterly* 82, no. 3 (September 1, 1967): 427–445.

Shin, Laura. *The Cryptopians: Idealism, Greed, Lies, and the Making of the First Big Cryptocurrency Craze*. New York: PublicAffairs, 2022. Kindle.

Simmel, Georg. "The Stranger." In *The Cultural Geography Reader*, edited by Tim Oakes and Patricia L. Price, 311–315. New York: Routledge, 2008.

Srinivasan, Balaji. *The Network State: How to Start a New Country*. Self-published, Amazon Kindle, 2022.

Stephenson, Neal. *The Diamond Age, or, Young Lady's Illustrated Primer*. New York: Bantam Books, 1995.

Suzor, Nicolas. "Digital Constitutionalism: Using the Rule of Law to Evaluate the Legitimacy of Governance by Platforms." *Social Media + Society* 4, no. 3 (July–September 2018): 1–11.

Swartz, Lana. "Blockchain Dreams: Imagining Techno-Economic Alternatives after Bitcoin." In *Another Economy Is Possible: Culture and Economy in a Time of Crisis*, edited by Manuel Castells, 82–105. Cambridge, UK: Polity, 2017.

Swartz, Lana. "Theorizing the 2017 Blockchain ICO Bubble as a Network Scam." *New Media and Society* 24, no. 7 (2022): 1695–1713.

Szabo, Nick. "Smart Contracts: Building Blocks for Digital Markets, Extropy." *Extropy: The Journal of Transhumanist Thought* 16, no. 18 (1996): 2–20.

Szabo, Nick. "The Idea of Smart Contracts." *Nick Szabo's Papers and Concise Tutorials* 6, no. 1 (1997): 199.

Szabo, Nick. "Money, Blockchains, and Social Scalability." Unenumerated, February 9, 2017. http://unenumerated.blogspot.com/2017/02/money-block chains-and-social-scalability.html.

Taleb, Nassim N. *The Black Swan: The Impact of the Highly Improbable*. London: Random House, 2017.

Tan, Joshua, Max Langenkamp, Anna Weichselbraun, Ann Brody, and Lucia Korpas. "Constitutions of Web3." Working paper, September 2023. https://constitutions.metagov.org/article.

Tomasello, Michael. *Why We Cooperate*. Cambridge, MA: MIT Press, 2009.

Tornado Cash. "Tornado.cash Is Finally Trustless!" Medium, May 20, 2022. https://tornado-cash.medium.com/tornado-cash-is-finally-trustless-a6e119 c1d1c2.

Vidan, Gili, and Vili Lehdonvirta. "Mine the Gap: Bitcoin and the Maintenance of Trustlessness." *New Media and Society* 21, no. 1 (January 2019): 42–59.

Voshmgir, Shermin. "Disrupting Governance with Blockchains and Smart Contracts." *Strategic Change* 26, no. 5 (2017): 499–509.

Walch, Angela. "On Code(rs) We Trust: Software Developers as Fiduciaries in Public Blockchains." In *Regulating Blockchain: Techno-Social and Legal Challenges*, edited by Philipp Hacker, Ioannis Lianos, Georgios Dimitropoulos, and Stefan Eich, 58–82. Oxford: Oxford University Press, 2019.

Waldron, Jeremy. "The Rule of Law and the Importance of Procedure." *Nomos* 50 (2011): 3–31.

Winner, Langdon. "Do Artifacts Have Politics?" *Daedalus* 109, no. 1 (Winter 1980): 121–136.

Wood, Gavin. "Ethereum: A Secure Decentralised Generalised Transaction Ledger—EIP 150 Revision." Yellow paper, 2014. https://gavwood.com/paper .pdf.

Wood, Gavin. "Allegality: Systems That Can't Care." YouTube video, 26:30. May 14, 2015. https://www.youtube.com/watch?v=Zh9BxYTSrGU.

Yeung, Karen. "Regulation by Blockchain: The Emerging Battle for Supremacy between the Code of Law and Code as Law." *Modern Law Review* 82, no. 2 (2019): 210.

Zargham, Michael. "Sensor Networks and Social Choice." Working paper, 2019. https://github.com/BlockScience/conviction/blob/master/social-sensorfu sion.pdf.

Zheng, Zibin, Shaoan Xie, Hong-Ning Dai, Weili Chen, Xiangping Chen, Jian Weng, and Muhammad Imran. "An Overview on Smart Contracts: Challenges, Advances and Platforms." *Future Generation Computer Systems* 105 (2020): 475–491.

Zuboff, Shoshana. *The Age of Surveillance Capitalism: The Fight for a Human Future at the New Frontier of Power*. London: Profile Books, 2019.

FURTHER READING

Allen, Darcy, Chris Berg, and Aaron Lane. *Cryptodemocracy: How Blockchain Can Radically Expand Democratic Choice*. Lanham, MD: Lexington Books, 2019.

Brekke, Jaya Klara. "Hacker-Engineers and Their Economies: The Political Economy of Decentralised Networks and 'Cryptoeconomics.'" *New Political Economy* 26, no. 4 (2021): 646–659. https://doi.org/10.1080/13563467.2020.1806223.

Buterin, Vitalik. *Proof of Stake*. New York: Seven Stories Press, 2022.

De Filippi, Primavera, and Aaron Wright. *Blockchain and the Law: The Rule of Code*. Cambridge, MA: Harvard University Press, 2018.

Dyzenhaus, David. *Legality and Legitimacy: Carl Schmitt, Hans Kelsen and Herman Heller in Weimar*. Oxford: Oxford University Press, 1997.

DuPont, Quinn. *Cryptocurrencies and Blockchains*. London: John Wiley & Sons, 2019.

Finck, Michèle. *Blockchain Regulation and Governance in Europe*. Cambridge: Cambridge University Press, 2018.

Hardin, Russell. *Trust & Trustworthiness*. New York: Russell Sage Foundation, 2004.

Kavanagh, Donncha, and Paul Dylan-Ennis, "Cryptocurrencies and the Emergence of Blockocracy." *The Information Society* 36, no. 5 (2020): 290–300. https://doi.org/10.1080/01972243.2020.1795958.

Kelsen, Hans. *Pure Theory of Law*. Clark, NJ: The Lawbook Exchange, 2005.

Lessig, Lawrence. *Code: And Other Laws of Cyberspace*. New York: Basic Books, 2009.

Lindahl, Hans. *Fault Lines of Globalization: Legal Order and the Politics of A-Legality*. Oxford: Oxford University Press, 2013.

Luhmann, Niklas. "Familiarity, Confidence, Trust: Problems and Alternatives." In *Trust: Making and Breaking Cooperative Relations*, edited by Diego Gambetta, 94–107. Oxford: Oxford University Press, 2000.

Ostrom, Elinor. *Governing the Commons: The Evolution of Institutions for Collective Action*. Cambridge: Cambridge University Press, 1990.

Pettit, Philip. "The Cunning of Trust." *Philosophy & Public Affairs* 24, no. 3 (1995): 202–225. https://doi.org/10.1111/j.1088-4963.1995.tb00029.x.

Schmitt, Carl. *Political Theology: Four Chapters on the Concept of Sovereignty*. Chicago: University of Chicago Press, 2005.

Werbach, Kevin. *The Blockchain and the New Architecture of Trust*. Cambridge, MA: MIT Press, 2018.

Yeung, Karen. "Regulation by Blockchain: The Emerging Battle for Supremacy between the Code of Law and Code as Law." *Modern Law Review* 82, no. 2 (2019): 207–239.

INDEX

The letter *f* following a page number denotes a figure.

PRIMAVERA DE FILIPPI is a research director at the National Center of Scientific Research in Paris, and faculty associate at the Berkman-Klein Center for Internet & Society at Harvard. Her research focuses on the legal challenges and opportunities of the metaverse, Web3, blockchain technology, and artificial intelligence. She is the coauthor of the book *Blockchain and the Law*, published in 2018 by Harvard University Press, and she was recently awarded a €2 million grant from the European Research Council to investigate how blockchain technology can help improve institutional governance through greater confidence and trust.

WESSEL REIJERS is a postdoctoral researcher at the Department of Philosophy, University of Vienna. Wessel's current research explores the impacts of emerging technologies on citizenship, most notably coming from social credit systems. Additionally, he explores the nature of distributed governance, investigating its potential as well as its pitfalls. He is the coauthor of *Narrative and Technology Ethics* and coeditor of the edited volume *Interpreting Technology*.

MORSHED MANNAN is a postdoctoral research fellow at the Robert Schuman Centre for Advanced Studies, European University Institute. Morshed is currently conducting interdisciplinary research on blockchain governance and regulation, platform cooperatives, and data cooperatives. He is currently exploring the application of constitutional and corporate governance theories to blockchain governance. He is the coeditor of the edited volume *Log Out_A Glossary of Technological Resistance and Decentralization*, a coauthor of the *COALA DAO Model Law*, and a coauthor of *Freedom of Establishment for Companies in Europe (EU/EEA)*.